The *Myth* of
ADOLESCENCE

CHILDHOOD
INNOCENCE

Raising
Responsible
Children
in an
Irresponsible
Society

ADULTHOOD
ACCOUNTABILITY

Dr. David Alan Black

DAVIDSON
PRESS
Yorba Linda, CA

The *Myth* of ADOLESCENCE

Raising *Responsible* Children in an *Irresponsible* Society

CHILDHOOD
INNOCENCE

ADULTHOOD
ACCOUNTABILITY

Dr. David Alan Black

The Myth of Adolescence™
Copyright © 1999 Dr. David Alan Black.
ALL RIGHTS RESERVED INTERNATIONALLY.

Edition 1
Version Number: 1.00
Build Number: 1
Build Date: 01 January 1999

Reference Number: 1
Release Date: 15 April 1999
CAM Format: Logos, PDF, STEP, XML
Document Format: MS Word 97 SR-1

Library of Congress Catalog Card Number: 98-89234
ISBN 1-891833-51-0 Hardback US$18.95

Cover Design: Larry Vilott (copyright © 1999
Davidson Press, Inc.). Layout: Charles Welty &
Larry Vilott. Document Processing: Charles
Welty.

23621 La Palma Avenue, #H460
Yorba Linda, CA 92887-5536
email: info@davidsonpress.com

Table of Contents

PUBLISHER'S PREFACE

You will either love this book, or you will hate it. There is no middle ground. Dr. David Alan Black shatters the most common theories that have shaped our nation and our world for over a century. His premise is quite simple: Adolescence is a social theory, and it is seriously flawed. Dr. Black says the concept of adolescence is relatively new, only about one hundred years old. Prior to that, a young person was considered to be an adult by the age of thirteen.

Further, Dr. Black says that the Bible has nothing to say about adolescence. That's because adolescence is foreign to the Bible. The Bible only speaks about responsibility, Dr. Black says. When you take responsibility away from young people and put them into a "twilight zone" between childhood and adulthood, grave consequences will result. The biblical pattern, Dr. Black says, is for responsibility to begin at the age of thirteen, or earlier (at the age of twelve) if the young person can handle it.

This compact volume opens the door to all sorts of discussions. At what age should a young person be employed? At what age should a young person marry? What if a young person commits a serious crime at the age of fourteen or fifteen? Should he or she face adult penalties for adult crimes, even the death penalty?

The *Myth of Adolescence* is just a beginning, the starting gate of what will be a new frontier for many people. But in reality, it's an old frontier, tried and proven over many centuries. It merely awaits discovery anew within these pages.

Charles Welty, *Publisher*

INTRODUCTION

In the only New Testament passage that mentions an incident from the childhood of Jesus, he was in trouble with his parents. Jesus had remained in Jerusalem without telling them what he was going to do. After a three-day search, his mother confronted him. "Son," she asked, "why have you treated us this way? Your father and I have been worried sick looking for you!" (Luke 2:48). Sound familiar? What young person hasn't been similarly confronted by an exasperated parent? "We've been worried about you. Couldn't you have called and told us you were going to stay late? How could you do this to us?"

Jesus' response was no less familiar: "Didn't you know that I had to be in my Father's house?" (Luke 2:49). What parent has never heard his or her child utter a similar lament? "You don't understand me. You just don't understand!"

Luke continues his account: "But they didn't understand what he said to them" (Luke 2:50). Young Jesus was making a tremendous theological statement in this passage, and it flew right past his parents' ability to comprehend. What parent has never found it difficult to understand his or her child? "You just aren't making any sense," we plead in frustration.

Imagine! *The Word became flesh and pitched his tent among us.* God was given armpits, elbows, two kidneys, and a navel. His legs grew, his voice cracked, his beard sprouted, his muscles hardened. He both frustrated and pleased his parents. "God's favor was with him" (Luke 2:40), and he gradually developed into a mature, responsible adult.

This book is about raising children to be like Jesus: mature and responsible adults. It was written out of love for

v

Christ, who not only modeled growth from childhood to adulthood, but who also loved and called children to himself. My basic thesis is that the earthly life of Christ is the perfect model for our own children's development from childhood to adulthood. As the sinless God-Man, Jesus uniquely shows us how our children can grow "in wisdom and maturity, and in favor with God and people" (Luke 2:52).

Regrettably, a great deal of misunderstanding and indifference has surrounded this crucial subject. From an expository point of view, next to nothing has been written on the topic of Jesus' human development and its bearing on child rearing. To my knowledge, no book in any language fully expounds all the New Testament passages regarding Jesus' developmental transitions, which is hardly believable when one considers the importance the Bible puts on these facts. Hopefully, this book will not only fulfill a need for Bible exposition, but will inspire parents to search the vast treasure of God's Word on their own. Precious truths, no doubt, still await discovery.

I urge you, at some point in your study of parenting, to look up all the Scripture passages cited in this book. It will not be an unprofitable task. On the contrary, reading God's Word will transform your thinking about the nature of human development and Christian parenting. It will expose false traditions and attitudes that drastically need changing. It will uplift your spirit and give you greater confidence in the truth of the Bible.

For ease of understanding, this book is divided into three parts. Part One, "Understanding Human Growth," presents an overview of the human life cycle in an easy-to-follow topical arrangement. In systematic fashion, it exposes the fallacy of adolescence and presents the essential elements of human growth and development from childhood to adulthood.

Part Two, "Parenting Principles from the Life of Jesus," is the heart of the book. If fair, reverent, and accurate exposition of God's Word will not convince parents of biblical child-rearing, then nothing will. Therefore this section includes an exposition of all relevant New Testament texts regarding the human life cycle. It shows how teenagers *are* open to (and even desirous of) growth and change, and how parents can be the primary change-agents in the home.

Finally, Part Three, "On to Maturity," outlines general ideas and specific advice for parents who seek to implement biblical principles of child-rearing. This is a how-to section that gives specific steps to help parents cope with the task of raising children to become responsible teenagers and adults. The guidelines are offered for parents who want to build relationships with their teenagers so that crises do *not* occur.

My prayer for this book—without apologies—is that the Divine Surgeon will use it as a delicate scalpel to restore sight. It has been written with practical concerns in mind and in language that virtually any parent can understand. Every effort has also been made to ensure that, in simplifying the terminology, the issues themselves are not oversimplified. My hope is that parents who desire to make the teen years positive for the teen and for the entire family will be able to implement these concepts to make relationships healthier and more productive.

Like my other forays into writing, this book was formed in a very common crucible, a busy (occasionally hectic) home. It was written in the daily process of rearing two active sons, as well as chickens, horses, goats, turkeys, and shelties, not to mention a constant stream of friends too numerous to name. Like many of you, my wife and I have endured the pains and pleasures of parenting in the midst of extremely busy careers. The very fact that this volume was ever written is a minor miracle from the hands of the

One who originated the whole idea of the family—and parenting.

I owe a special word of appreciation to my friends of the "Breakfast Club." Chum and Dave, you were my sounding board for many of the issues addressed in this book, and I'm grateful for your honest responses and loving encouragement. To my parents-in-law, Brad and Betty Lapsley, goes my appreciation for taking the time to discuss parts of the manuscript with me. My teaching assistants at Southeastern Seminary, Don Brown and Chris Thompson, did an outstanding job of typing, and their labor of love is deeply appreciated. Finally, I owe a special debt of thanks to the sons of my youth for having taught me much of what is in these pages. Nate and Matt, you are not only my earthly sons and spiritual brothers in Christ, but my closest friends. I am a father singularly blessed!

I gratefully dedicate this book to my wife Becky, whose joyful, demanding, and ever-deepening relationships with our two sons embody all of the principles in these pages. She has made a tremendous commitment to our children, requiring not only personal sacrifice and great love, but also exhausting amounts of her time and energy daily. I never cease to marvel at her capacity to give so much of herself to them—and me. In fact, if you could *see* her relationships with our sons, I would not need to *write* on this subject at all. The day will surely come when her sons will "rise up and call her blessed."

Truly, this book has been a joint effort. Thank you, Becky. I love you.

The *Myth* of

ADOLESCENCE

Raising
Responsible
Children
in an
Irresponsible
Society

Dr. David Alan Black

Part One:

Understanding Human Growth

Chapter 1:   GOD'S PATTERN FOR HUMAN GROWTH

Jesus, Our Model and Hope

This book is about your child's growth, that is, about the maturing of his or her mind, character, and personality. It is based on the conviction that the earthly life of Jesus provides a perfect yet supremely practical model of human development. According to Luke 2:52, growth was a process for Jesus. At the significant transitional age of twelve, on the brink of young adulthood, Jesus "grew in wisdom and maturity, and in favor with God and people." The cycles of normal human development applied to Jesus' mental, physical, spiritual, and social development.

Some may think that to speak of Jesus' human development in this way is to minimize his divine nature. As I have spoken to others about the topic of the humanity of Christ, I have more than once heard the comment: "This sounds interesting, but is all of this really necessary to understand who Jesus really is?" This question does not spring from any polemical intentions. On the contrary, people are justifiably wary of any form of teaching that might undermine the deity of Christ. I share that concern. As important as understanding the earthly life of Christ is, it can actually hamper biblical faith if the approach becomes a kind of intellectualism that is irrelevant or peripheral to Christian faith.

The full deity of Christ is everywhere declared in the New Testament. The apostle John wrote, "In the beginning, the Word existed. The Word was with God, and the Word was God" (John 1:1). Thomas, another of Jesus' disciples, exclaimed, "My Lord and my God!" (John 20:28). The apostle

1

Paul asserted, "To them belong the patriarchs, and from them, according to the flesh, Christ descended, who is God over all, blessed forever! Amen" (Romans 9:5). The same apostle later wrote that we "wait for the blessed hope and the glorious appearance of our great God and Savior, Jesus Christ" (Titus 2:13). The author of Hebrews states, "But about the Son he says, 'Your throne, O God, is forever and ever'" (Hebrews 1:8). Likewise, the apostle Peter writes to "those who have obtained a faith that is as valuable as ours through the righteousness of our God and Savior, Jesus Christ" (2 Peter 1:1).

Therefore, in what follows in this book, please do not think for a moment that I am minimizing the deity of Christ in any way, shape, or form. When properly understood, however, the Bible's assertion that Jesus developed as a human being does not detract from his deity. The Scriptures declare that Jesus is the God-Man: 100% God and 100% man. Thus his sinlessness and holiness do not lessen his true humanity. The apostle Paul suggests that Jesus, as a servant, was willing to forgo the full use of his divine powers (Philippians 2:7), and so a normal human development is not ruled out. Like the boy Samuel (1 Samuel 2:26) and the responsible son in Proverbs 3:4, Jesus matured into a person both God and people approved of. For thirty-three years he would feel everything you and I have ever felt.

No one has put this better than Max Lucado:

> It is much easier to keep the humanity out of the incarnation. Clean the manure from around the manger. Wipe the sweat out of his eyes. Pretend he never snored or blew his nose or hit his thumb with a hammer.
>
> He's easier to stomach that way. There is something about keeping him divine that keeps him distant, packaged, predictable.

2

But don't do it. For heaven's sake, don't. Let him be as human as he intended to be. Let him into the mire and muck of our world. For only if we let him in can he pull us out.[1]

As Christian parents, it is vitally important that we acknowledge the relevance of the earthly life of Jesus to the task of child-rearing. The physical manifestations of God in the Old Testament were only preliminary ways of preparing for the highest physical manifestation of God in the coming of Jesus Christ. So when we portray Jesus as an otherworldly character, we undermine the key concrete instance in which God "spoke" to us (Hebrews 1:1-4). Parents should not be afraid to stress the tangible acts of God in physical reality. Children need to know that God manifested himself in the flesh through a man called Jesus (1 Timothy 3:16). Paul describes this in Philippians 2:6-11:

> *In God's own form existed he,*
> *And shared with God equality,*
> *Deemed nothing needed grasping.*
> *Instead, poured out in emptiness,*
> *A servant's form did he possess,*
> *A mortal man becoming.*
> *In human form he chose to be,*
> *And lived in all humility,*
> *Death on a cross obeying.*
> *Now lifted up by God to heaven,*
> *A name above all others given,*
> *This matchless name possessing.*
> *And so, when Jesus' name is called,*
> *The knees of everyone should fall,*
> *Where'er they are residing.*

---

[1] Max Lucado, *God Came Near* (Portland, OR: Multnomah, 1987) pp. 26-27.

Then every tongue in one accord,
  Will say that Jesus Christ is Lord,
    While God the Father praising.

It is this Jesus, who "learned obedience through his sufferings" (Hebrews 5:8), who is the perfect pattern of human development. In his book *The Jesus Model*, David McKenna explains why this is of prime importance:

> Christian faith pivots on a person—Jesus of Nazareth.... As the Son of God, he claimed to be our Lord; as the Son of Man, he claimed to be our Model; and as fully God and fully man, he claimed to be our Redeemer.... In response, we cannot forget that Jesus' claim to be the Son of Man holds equal authority in the Christian portfolio. If Jesus was a real and complete man who participated fully in the human experience, then he must be our model and our hope. Anything less and the case for Christianity is dismissed.[2]

Yes, Jesus is our "model and hope"! To "be like him" (1 John 3:2), then, is a legitimate and valid goal of all Christians, even though in this life we will always fall short of exemplifying Christ perfectly.

The goal of this book is to offer practical help to parents who want their children to develop, like Jesus did, into mature and responsible adults. My desire is to lead you into a deeper understanding of who Jesus is and the manner in which he developed into manhood. Among other things, we will see that:

---

[2]David McKenna, *The Jesus Model* (Waco: Word, 1977) pp. 13-14 (italics added).

- Jesus, the Lord and Creator of all, went through normal cycles of human growth and development, just as we do today. In fact, as the perfect God-Man, Jesus is the ideal model of human development that is to be followed by all believers.

- The way in which Jesus was raised by Joseph and Mary provides today's parents with a sound and sensible model of Christian parenting. Joseph and Mary were meticulous about the way they brought up their son.

- Parental example and instruction was at the heart of all Jewish educational endeavors. Parents themselves oversaw the teaching and training of their children.

- The modern idea of adolescence as an irresponsible and topsy-turvy "time-out" between childhood and adulthood is unbiblical and destructive.

- Contrary to today's "me-first" culture, the knowledge of God and his ways was considered more important than the knowledge of one's self.

- Educating children for adulthood involved the essential two steps of giving them "roots" and "wings."

Above all, we will see the importance of providing the nurture our children need to grow strong enough to live in this world. And we will see the importance of granting our children progressively greater freedoms to allow them to mature into responsible adults.

This is how I want to raise my own children, and it is a tall order! Parenting is both terrific and terrifying—all at once. It is one of the hardest, most wonderful, most exasperating, most ennobling, most frustrating, most rewarding and exhilarating jobs of life.

Does the task look too full of obstacles? Let me give you some advice: *Parenting works for those who have the will to make it work.* Be prepared to make huge, sometimes unfairly huge, investments into the lives of your children—freely, joyously, generously, continually. For on the other side of sacrifice and hardship is greatness.

Understanding the Human Life Cycle

The first step on the road to effective parenting is understanding the basics of human growth and development. There is an old saying that children grow "by leaps and bounds." It really isn't true. Children grow gradually in steps and stages. Modern psychological studies have made parents sensitive to these steps and stages of children's development—perhaps too sensitive. A rigid view of developmental stages can easily become a kind of scientific straight jacket, implying that if a child is not "performing according to grade level" he or she is retarded.

Nevertheless, it is very helpful to know what psychologists are saying about how children can and do develop. It is not fair for Christians to acknowledge the advances that medical science has brought to children but insist that nothing can be learned from psychology. Some fundamental understandings of what children and youth are like, the problems they face, and the events that affect their lives are revealed by psychological studies. Sound biblical theology unites special revelation (the Bible) and the best of natural revelation (science), even if it always gives pride of place to the Scriptures.

An ideal theology of development would require the lifetime of a team of theologians and practitioners to produce an exhaustive study of all the stages from childhood to adulthood. The goal of this book is more modest: it will attempt only to make concrete suggestions about the essential facets of human development and their applications to the stages of a child's growth. I will use the term "life cycle" to refer to a person's development from birth to adulthood. The term "life cycle" suggests that life follows a basic sequence. It is a process or journey from a starting point (birth) to a termination point (death). Within this cycle are seasons or stages: a series of phases, each having its own distinguishing characteristics, like the acts of a play or the movements in a symphony. Each of these seasons is different from the one that precedes and follows it.

With Jesus as our model, let's look at the process of his own growth and development as a human being. The Scriptures relate three basic phases in Jesus' life cycle: (1) birth to twelve years (Luke 2:41-52); (2) twelve until Jesus' baptism at approximately age thirty (Luke 3:23); and (3) the period of Jesus' public ministry culminating in his death, resurrection, and ascension. This is not to deny that Jesus may have experienced other seasons of life that are emphasized in modern psychology. However, these are the only ones that the Bible emphasizes. They also correspond to what might be called the *major* phases of the life cycle. We can probably all agree without difficulty on a foundational phase ("childhood" or "pre-adulthood"), a transitional phase ("emerging adulthood"), and a mature phase ("senior adulthood"). These phases may be pictured as follows:

1. Childhood/Pre-Adulthood (ages 1-12)
2. Emerging Adulthood (ages 12-30)
3. Senior Adulthood (ages 30-death)

These phases describe the human life cycle in the broadest sense. They correspond exactly to the persons John describes as "little children," "young people," and "fathers" in 1 John 2:12-14—a passage that uniquely captures the idea of necessary phases of growth that can be arranged into a whole (see Chapter 3). Moreover, each phase has its own distinct and unifying qualities, which together constitute the journey from birth to death.

The transitions that occur between these phases of life are extremely significant. Puberty usually starts at twelve and provides a transition from childhood to adulthood. It begins with bodily changes leading to sexual maturity, but it involves several other important changes as well. At around thirty the young adult is ready to take his or her place as a full participant in the society of adults. Psychologists use age thirty as a reference point for studying the change from "novice adulthood" to a more "senior" position in work, family, and community. Researchers have also shown that the aging process begins around one's thirtieth birthday.

In terms of developmental tasks, at puberty the child is moving out of the pre-adult world and is making a preliminary step into adulthood. The basic developmental tasks of this phase are exploring the possibilities of adult living, imagining oneself as a participant in the adult world, and learning how to make responsible choices in life. The transition at age thirty provides an opportunity to work on limitations and flaws in the first adult structure and to create a more responsible, meaningful, and satisfying lifestyle. This is a time to ask, "What is really important in life? What's inappropriate that I want to remove from my life?"

Finally, during the senior adulthood phase a person enters the settling down period of his or her life calendar. The basic developmental tasks of this period are finding a niche in society, changing from an "amateur" adult to one more firmly accepted and respected, and becoming a senior member in one's world with a greater measure of authority. The added responsibility that comes with senior adulthood means that more and more of one's "little child" has to be surrendered.

This sequence of phases forms the basic scaffold of the life cycle as presented in the Scriptures. Within this framework we will pursue the fundamental question of this book: *As Christian parents, what can we learn about child-rearing from the process of Jesus' development from childhood to adulthood?* We will discover important clues as to the nature of this development in Luke's description of Jesus' "Age Twelve" (Luke 2:41-52) and "Age Thirty" transitions (Luke 3:23). To my knowledge, these vital transitions are discussed nowhere else in the massive literature on Christian parenting. Yet people generally live through these same developmental periods of life that are modeled for us by Christ himself.

If Christ's life is any example, parents are not left to grope in the darkness. A builder's son has shown us the way.

So who is he? Let's try to find out. Let's sit on the cold, hard floor of the home where he played. Let's smell the sawdust of the carpentry shop. Let's sigh as we see him close the shutters on the sunshine of his youth and say goodbye to Nazareth. Let's try to see him.

Roots and Wings

The evidence for stages of growth is substantial. The idea of stages suggests that life develops more like a stairway than an escalator. Effective parents understand their child's behavior and reasoning in terms of these stages.

Having discussed the stages of growth and their developmental objectives, how do we help our children reach these objectives, assuming that they, too, want to reach them? Here's my suggestion, and this is going to be the basis for all we do in raising our children:

Give them roots, and then give them wings!

That's the foundation, and we absolutely have to start there. This is what Jesus' parents did for him, and it is what we must do for our children.

Giving our children roots means that we ground them in the ways of God through nurture and discipline. Giving them wings means that we raise them to be independent, responsible adults. Thus, according to Scripture, *the basic task of parenting is to see that our children have a foundation that will enable them to make responsible decisions when they grow up.*

This book is all about roots and wings—nurturing children in the essentials of the Christian faith so that one day they can make their own mark on the world. This is what makes parenting a unique task. Its goal is to raise children who can think clearly, take responsibility for their own actions, and have the will to learn from their mistakes. We do that when we gradually allow our children to gain more and more control over their lives.

This is the way God operates. He loves us enough to allow us to make our own decisions. He loves us without being overprotective. He provides us, his children, with the resources we need to function successfully in the Christian life. Then he trains us through his Word so that we are able to use these resources profitably unto good works (2 Timothy 3:16-17).

Likewise, as our children grow up, we must make a transition to granting them the privilege and responsibility of making their own decisions and solving their own problems. God liberates his children to be real people, free to develop, to explore, to find themselves and his purpose for their lives. Should Christian parents do any less? Don't be surprised when a young person says, "Don't fence me in!" Wise parents are careful not to manipulate their children into following their own dreams.

In short, then, the challenge and blessing of parenting is to give children a chance to build a Christian orientation to life and then to love them enough to allow them to think and act for themselves. Allowing children at a young age to practice decision-making on simple issues teaches them to think, to control their own lives. The more decisions they make, the more responsible they become. We can give them guidance, but they must be taught to think for themselves.

Unfortunately, many parents are guilty of doing the opposite. They grant many privileges when their children are young, and then demand more and more control when they become teenagers. Some parents inadvertently develop a co-dependent relationship with their children. They receive gratification from this co-dependency and encourage it lest they lose their own sense of purpose and identity.

God's plan, however, is for parents to raise responsible children by letting them make an increasing number of decisions for themselves. Laying a firm foundation on the Word of God, setting realistic boundaries, then allowing choices—these are the ingredients for successful parenting. And the ultimate goal of parenting is letting our children go. *They need wings, not only roots.* They're not here to meet our needs but to fulfill the Master's plan for their lives—in their world, without us.

If we can teach our children this sense of responsibility to their Creator, then we have accomplished the major part of our parental task. This is summarized beautifully in a familiar Old Testament proverb: "Train up a child according to his way, and when he is old he will not depart from it" (Proverbs 22:6). Some interpreters think this verse means that we are to train our children in the ways of God (in his—*God's*—way). Others argue that we are to train them in keeping with their individual gifts or bent (in his—*the child's*—way). The debate is unnecessary, since both meanings are true. (Such intentional ambiguity is a common characteristic of Hebrew poetry.) Godly parents know the ways of God and pass these on to their children. They also raise their children with sensitivity to the design God has for each child individually.

To put it another way: It's a question of "roots" (*God's* way) and "wings" (the *child's* way).

These are the essential building blocks of parenting from the life and experience of Christ. In the world of first century Palestine, twelve year-old children were given a large amount of freedom and control over their lives. This instilled within them the sense of responsibility and maturity necessary to live in the real world. Similarly, the limits we set for our children's behavior are ever-expanding, offering more and more freedom as the years go by.

In the following chapters we will look at roots and wings—what they are, how they develop, and how they connect with the growth process. As you begin to practice these principles, bear in mind that God is concerned about more than how well we understand roots and wings. He is concerned about our *actions*. And in his Word, actions are clearly defined.

Chapter 2: EXPLODING THE MYTH OF ADOLESCENCE

The Invention of Adolescence

It was 6:20 a.m., July 29, 1995. Starting home from an overnight camping trip with seven friends, the young man lost control of his father's 1987 Chevy Suburban and sent it tumbling across a barren stretch of the Mojave Desert in Southern California. As the 5,000-pound truck rolled across the desert floor, the lives of four of his friends were snuffed out. "It's my fault," he told the survivors, sobbing. "I killed my friends!"

California Highway Patrol officers quickly agreed. The young man's breath reeked of beer, and a blood test showed that he was legally drunk. Had he been considered an adult, James Virgil Patterson probably would have been sent to prison, perhaps for years. But because he was two months shy of his eighteenth birthday, the law regarded him as an errant youth. Despite the fact that he admitted to killing his four friends and seriously injuring three others, the law exempted him from adult punishment. Instead, the San Bernardino County Juvenile Court sentenced him to 120 days in jail and 120 days of alcohol rehabilitation. (As a gesture to the parents, the court also barred him from taking part in graduation ceremonies at his high school.)[3]

This story, of course, isn't just about drinking and driving. It's a parable about parents and their lost teenagers—young men and women who, because they are considered "adolescents," are excused from personal responsibility by a

---

[3]See *Los Angeles Times Magazine*, July 28, 1996, pp. 10-12.

13

society that seems at a loss as to how to deal with its teen-agers.

In dealing with the subject of adolescence, it may be helpful to begin with a few definitions. Etymologically, the terms "adolescent" and "adult" are closely related. The Latin term "adolescent" originally meant "growing one" and generally referred to the sudden spurt of growth at the age of puberty (around twelve or thirteen years of age). The word "adult" meant "grown one" and referred to a person who had passed his or her growth spurt. In essence, then, an "adult" was a person who was able to have children. Thus, throughout history, puberty was the beginning of adulthood itself, not the beginning of a stage between childhood and adulthood.

The problem is that our modern American society generally considers an "adult" to be a person who has "come of age" (this "age" of adulthood being variously defined), not necessarily a person who is sexually mature. This separation of the two meanings of "adult" has given us the modern concept of "adolescence." According to David Bakan:

> The idea of adolescence as an intermediary period of life starting at puberty... is the product of modern times.... [It] developed in the latter half of the nineteenth century and the early twentieth century... to prolong the years of childhood.[4]

Thus, the term "adolescence" now refers to the teen years, during which teenagers are treated as children even though they are really "adults" in the original sense of the word.

Bakan identifies three developments in American society that made adolescence an officially recognized period in

---

[4]David Bakan, "Adolescence in America: From Idea to Social Fact," *Daedalus* 100 (1971) pp. 979-995.

the human life cycle. First, compulsory education laws were passed that removed the decision about whether a child should be educated away from parents. Education was mandated by law, and parents could be punished for keeping their children out of school. Of course, for thousands of years prior to this, parents educated their own children. They taught them whatever was needed to succeed in society. In biblical times, Hebrew parents were responsible for the education of their children. Roman parents did the same. Modern laws mandating school attendance began in Germany in the seventeenth century, though the laws were seldom enforced since parents viewed those laws as the state trying to do what they should do. Gradually, laws were passed in the United States that required all children to go to school. In fact, the high school is a part of our society's invention of adolescence. With these changes, adults ("adolescents") and not just children were forced to attend school.

Second, child labor laws were enacted that made it illegal to employ persons below certain ages. This served to lengthen the period of childhood since early teenagers, for example, could no longer work full time. The result was to make young people economically dependent. They were not allowed to work, so they did not have their own money to spend. However, for thousands of years it was not this way. Young people worked with their parents or beside a master as an apprentice until they could become independent. In nineteenth century Massachusetts, for example, young people over twelve were expected to support themselves.

Finally, as we have seen, a juvenile justice system was created to segregate younger lawbreakers from older ones. This produced a different system of record keeping, punishment, and probation for "juveniles." Just as teenagers were no longer expected to be responsible to support themselves, they were no longer held responsible for their criminal acts, despite the fact that for thousands of years the legal system treated teenagers as adults. In nineteenth century America a fifteen-year-old lawbreaker could be punished the same way as a thirty-five-year-old offender would be. Today, however, our laws have turned adults into children. As a result, all too many young people are literally "getting away with murder."

The intrusion of legal adolescence into American society was fairly well established by the early part of the twentieth century and quickly began to influence how young people grew up. By the 1920s the marriage age, along with inauguration into the work force, was steadily moving upward. Young people were "protected" from environments that "forced" maturity on them. Instead, they lived in a period of extended childhood. For the first time in history, young people were not allowed to make adult decisions at the age of puberty. Adolescence became a "psychological moratorium," a delaying of adult commitments. As a result, permissiveness and playfulness were encouraged.[5] There even developed organizations to turn youth from adults into children. With the invention of the Boy Scouts, the Girl Scouts, and boys' and girls' agricultural clubs, adults officially began calling people in their teens "boys" and "girls."

Adolescence, or "adolescentism," as one could call it (since it is a social theory and not a fact), burst with a shower of sparks on the Western world in the early 1900s and is clearly here to stay. It is an obvious challenge to Christian morality that, if accepted, would sweep away most of the approach and conclusions for which this book contends. It is time for serious Christians to take a long hard look at it.

---

[5]For a description of adolescence as a psychological moratorium, see E. Erickson, *Identity, Youth, and Crisis* (New York: W. W. Norton and Co., 1968) p. 157.

It is my conviction that the social theory of adolescence undermines both the Christian understanding of human nature and the way in which Christians analyze moral thought. It underscores the modern disinclination to treat a person as responsible for his or her actions. When we assert the "fact" that teenagers are to act like children rather than like adults, it becomes a self-fulfilling prophecy.

The issue of premarital sex is an obvious case in point.[6] The ancient Hebrews were not only allowed to marry at puberty, they were encouraged to do so. Their reasoning was simple: if people did not marry at puberty, premarital sex would become a problem. Rabbi Hisda, for example, boasted that he had married at sixteen, though he thought it would have been better to have married at fourteen since he would have avoided two years of impure thoughts.[7]

Under Roman law (2,000 years ago), women could marry at twelve and men at fourteen. A thousand years ago this was true under English law as well. Two hundred years ago in the United States it was still the same: women could marry at twelve and men at fourteen. For at least three thousand years, the minimum legal age for marriage stayed the same. People accepted teen marriage and saw it as the best solution to the problem of premarital sex.

Now let me hasten to add that I'm not suggesting young people get married as teenagers. Today more than half of all teen marriages end in divorce, though obviously the problem is not just age but involves other factors as well. In fact, one might argue that it is precisely because of the invention of adolescence that many teenagers are not socially mature enough for marriage. Perhaps if our society

---

[6]See further Ronald Kotesky, *Understanding Adolescence* (Wheaton: Victor, 1987) pp. 14-15.

[7]See the Talmud, *Kiddushin* 29b-30a.

had expected them to act like responsible adults, many of them would be mature enough to marry.

My point is that, by creating adolescence, our society requires our teens to be *celibate* (to abstain from marriage) without at the same time encouraging them to be *chaste* (to abstain from sexual relations). In other words, young people are not allowed to express their God-given sexual desires in marriage, yet at the same time they are not taught to control those desires. In fact, just the opposite set of values is encouraged. The worlds of advertising, television, and popular culture all communicate that sex can be engaged in strictly for pleasure by any physically mature person. The result is that, while most teenagers are unmarried, most do not abstain from sexual activity.[8]

The issue of compulsory education is another example of the problems adolescence has created. There is nothing inherently wrong with being in school for 180 days a year for six hours a day for ten years. The problem is that compulsory education laws say that young people must spend a given amount of time in school, not that they must learn. It is all too tempting for youth to simply put in their time, rather than learn. It is tragic to see how many parents in American society have remanded the responsibility for the moral education of their children to the public school, which is unqualified to teach morality because it has rejected all responsibility for inculcating moral values and character building and, in many cases, actually teaches against morality. John Dewey, the humanist educator, has had more influence on our public schools than many parents are willing to acknowledge. Believing that humanism is good, he de-

---

[8]Currently, American sex education programs fall into two categories: those that promote the fallacy of "safe sex," and those that encourage abstinence. Among the latter are James Dobson's "Family Values and Sex Education," Josh McDowell's "Why wait?" programs, and the Southern Baptist Convention's "True Love Waits."

cided to gain control of the schools and train a whole new generation of youth. The result was predictable: schools without learning, graduates without education, and rebels drifting aimlessly through life.

Clearly, the invention of adolescence has altered the process of growing up in America. When school, church, and family treat sixteen-year-olds like young children, teenagers act in ways that justify that treatment. Little wonder today's young people are suffering from role confusion. They don't know who they are, where they came from, or where they are headed. They are at the starting gate of life with no place to go. Since the gate will not be opened for another six to ten years, the results of such frustration are predictable. In fact, today we are witnessing a situation in which teens sport an identity confusion openly and almost mockingly.

If we are to understand parenting we must begin by taking seriously this matter of adolescence. If Christian parenting is to be biblical, false traditions and misconceptions that have obscured child rearing must be challenged and exposed in the pure light of God's truth. The basic assumption underpinning this book is that Holy Scripture is the surest foundation and blueprint upon which to build parenting reform, renewal, and revitalization. Reformation of Christian parenting can only begin when the distorted structure of human tradition is dismantled and replaced by a general return to biblical origins. Such a reformation is not only possible, but absolutely essential.

The Bible and Adolescence

What, then, do the Scriptures say about adolescence? *Absolutely nothing.* In the Bible, people went directly from childhood to adulthood. Moses, for example, is never referred to as an adolescent. In Exodus 2 he is called a "child" in verse 10, and by verse 11 he had "grown up." Here we might have expected to find a reference to a period between childhood and adulthood, but such a reference is absent. The same contrast between the "child" Moses and the "grown up" Moses is found in Hebrews 11:23-24: "By faith Moses was hidden by his parents for three months after he was born, because they saw that he was a beautiful *child*, and were not afraid of the king's order. By faith Moses, when he had *grown up*, refused to be called a son of Pharaoh's daughter." Adolescence simply did not exist among the ancient Hebrews.

And what do we find in the New Testament? When the apostle Paul described his own development, he talked about childhood and manhood: "When I was a child, I spoke like a child, thought like a child, and reasoned like a child. When I became a man, I gave up my childish ways" (1 Corinthians 13:11). Notice that the major differences Paul mentions are in language, thinking, and reasoning. In these areas he went from being a child to being an adult, without an intervening period of "adolescence." Moreover, when the apostle John described people at different stages of maturity, he talked about "little children," "young people," and "fathers" (1 John 2:12-14). The "young people" were not really adolescents but young *men and women*.

Moses, Paul, John, and others at that time went directly from childhood to adulthood. *They were teenagers, but they were never adolescents.* Although the Bible talks about teenagers, it treats them like adults, not like children. Today, however, we have invented a period during which childhood and adulthood overlap. No longer is there a definitive transition between these stages of life. This invention of adolescence has created enormous problems in the areas of identity, sexuality, work, and school.

I can't believe the books on child-rearing I've read that say, "You have to treat your adolescents as much like children as possible. Don't confuse them by expecting adult behavior." One Christian father, for example, has written:

> Unfortunately, our culture forces teenagers' development too rapidly.... With my own teens I felt that slowing down their adolescence was a positive thing and so I very consciously insulated my teens from the fast pace of growth that adolescent culture assumes. One way I did this was by not letting them get their driver's licenses until they were out of high school.[9]

Although I empathize with this parent's struggle with "adolescent culture," this seems to be an ill-advised means of handling the problem.

A different approach is suggested by Ronald Kotesky:

> The basic thing you can do to help your adolescents now is to treat them as much like adults as possible.... Even if other people expect your teenagers to act irresponsibly, you can expect them to be responsible.[10]

This is precisely the point of the biblical texts we looked at above: *parents are to expect the best from their teenagers.* If we allow them to act like irresponsible children, they will. On the other hand, if we expect them to act like responsible adults, as people did for thousands of years, they will.

Some parents may object, "Our children are only in their early teens. That's too young to expect them to behave as responsible adults." I disagree. On the one hand, it's clear

---

[9]Larry Richards, "The Stages of Adolescence," in Jay Kesler (ed.), *Parents and Teenagers* (Wheaton: Victor, 1984) p. 157.

[10]Ronald Kotesky, *Understanding Adolescence* (Wheaton: Victor, 1987) pp. 20-21.

that our modern philosophy of treating teenagers like children is not working. On the other hand, if you do not expect responsible behavior from them now, when will you? When they go off to college? (If you do not help them develop self-discipline when they are still at home, they will not know how to study.) When they get married? (If you do not expect responsible behavior toward the opposite sex now, you will be making their adjustment to marriage in the future all that more difficult.) When they get a job? (Teenagers who have not learned how to work from their parents are frequently ill-prepared for the job market.)

Now, I'm not saying that we should impose adulthood on our children before they are able to handle it. The basic gift of childhood is innocence and carefree play. There is something horribly wrong when young children are used by adults as status symbols, when they become the decision-makers in the home, when they become therapists to dysfunctional parents. Kids should be kids, and children should be allowed to play. But I'm not talking about your thirteen- or fourteen-year-old; I'm talking about pre-teens.

So let's be clear on one thing: *According to the Bible, the teen era is not a "time-out" between childhood and adulthood.* It is not primarily a time of horseplay, of parties, of sports, of games. It is not a period of temporary insanity between childhood and adulthood. The Bible treats teens as responsible adults, and so should we. Paul told Timothy, a young man, "Don't let anyone look down on you because you are young. Instead be an example for other believers in your speech, behavior, love, faith, and purity" (1 Timothy 4:12). Though still young, Timothy was to speak, act, love, believe, and relate to the opposite sex in such a way that others would look at his life and want to be just like him!

Do we expect *our* teenagers to be examples? The law may not allow them to marry or work, but we can help them become responsible partners in a family relationship.

Our expectations as parents are the most important factors in getting our teenagers to act like responsible adults. Expecting the best from our teenagers, doing things with them, and sharing our understanding with them will not automatically make the teen years painless, but it will make the task of growing up easier.

Dealing with a Secular Culture

In a non-believing and religiously pluralistic society like ours, even young children become aware that there are people who believe differently from themselves and their parents. The truth is that the concept of teenage responsibility is widely unpopular today, even in some churches and youth groups. Today we just accept the "fact" that teenagers are to act like children rather than like adults. Since we do not want them to grow up too fast, they don't.

In the general culture, we have a group of parents who grew up in the permissive 1960s. Their attitudes toward drugs, sex, authority, and education are vastly different than those of their own parents. Many of these parents naively assume that the schools will teach their children responsibility. Unfortunately, Christian parents can fall into the same trap. For many, faith in Christ is merely a ticket to heaven. We've side-stepped the idea of responsibility and the behavioral implications of Christianity. Therefore, Christian youth often share the same worldly outlook of non-Christians. They look at sexuality, for example, like any other physical urge. "If it itches, scratch it" becomes their philosophy. And they don't feel guilty in the least about it.

Christian parents, however, *can* make a difference. They can say, "Hey, we've had *enough*! We're going to do something about this as a family." They can decide to act on Christian principles, principles that are sometimes opposed even by their pastors and youth leaders. The idea of God expecting teenagers to behave responsibly may seem illogical to some, but we need to teach our sons and daughters to be biblically-oriented in their thinking.

In closing this chapter I would like to offer four practical suggestions for preparing your children for adulthood. These suggestions will form the foundation for much of what we have to say later in this book.

First of all, now that you have a biblical understanding of adolescence, *share that insight with your own children*. Show them how the concept of adulthood has changed over the years, and how they are caught in a situation that society has forced on all of you. Explain to them that they cannot blindly accept all the signals that their culture gives them about their identity. These signals are frequently conflicting and, if taken at face value, can contribute to a sense of inner confusion. Then begin to share with your children the prospect of their own rite of passage into adulthood. Naturally, if you have been treating your teenagers like children, they will need help in gradually assuming responsibility. You cannot just suddenly tell them to act like adults. If possible, begin by providing your young children with experiences in independence. Staying overnight with grandma and grandpa is a good start. Later, caring for pets or handling money helps, too. But the truth is, you can't do it overnight. You start when your children are small and gradually increase their responsibility.

Second, *avoid establishing overly rigid boundaries in your homes*. Parents can easily overreact in their desire to protect their children and themselves. The doors to their homes stay locked, the people inside are afraid to step outside, and they're embarrassed to let outsiders see what goes on within their four walls. They succeed in sheltering their children from many of the bad things in the world, but they also keep them from experiencing learning opportunities and enjoyable activities. Eventually their children grow up and are unable to make sound decisions about what people are safe and what activities are good for them. Consequently, they get into trouble. Perhaps you need to develop more of a sense of community by interacting with the outside world and by becoming more hospitable in your home.

Third, I want to emphasize the need to *be realistic when discussing culture with our children*. The current social setting in America is beyond our control. Our culture has created adolescence and has handed it on to us. Unless the culture radically changes, the teen years will still continue to be a time when young people may not vote, marry, or obtain meaningful work. Perhaps someday in the future teenagers may be treated like responsible adults rather than like children, but for now we must struggle with adolescence. Our culture leaves us no choice. It is therefore important to identify the social situation facing the teenagers we are concerned about, for we cannot influence them unless we enter sympathetically into their world.

Finally, you should *be aware that our society's concept of adolescence can introduce tension into the process of parenting*. One area of tension is the extended period of preparation from the end of childhood to the start of an adult vocation. Young people from eighteen to the beginning of their vocation are often called "kids," even though a more appropriate term would be "young adults." Teens rightly object to this kind of treatment.

A second area of tension involves the issue of dependency. Even after graduating from high school, many young people continue to live at home and are under the supervision of their parents. There is evidence that this type of dependency is a possible source of hostility that needs to be acknowledged and dealt with.

A third area of tension is the challenge posed by the contemporary youth culture, which encourages young people to express their hopes, fears, and frustrations in ways that are often ungodly. Music, dance, entertainment, and clothing are ways of expressing the marginal status of youth in society. During the teen years especially, when young adults are told they are not needed by society, they have a special need to belong to a community. Thus, while waiting for "adult status" as defined by their culture, they need to have a sense of belonging to a group of people they respect and from whom they can receive recognition. If adults make the church a community to which young people want to belong, they will be helping teenagers move more smoothly into adulthood. Life together as the people of God can provide an extended family in which youth can work out issues of identity and intimacy. The Body of Christ can be a significant factor in the moral and spiritual development of youth at any age.

In conclusion, parents have the unenviable position of being the focal point in a conflict between teenagers and their culture. We are responsible for supporting our teens and keeping them in school until the adult world has a place for them. In the meantime, the best thing we can do is to treat our adolescents like adults. Later on we will have some specific suggestions on how to do this, but the commitment must begin now.

As you begin this process, my advice is to *be optimistic*. God never asks us to do what we can not do, though we must rely totally on his strength. Remember, "The one who is in you is greater than the one who is in the world." (1 John 4:4). If we will put our faith to work—not just as a way to heaven, but as a way of life—then it becomes powerful!

Chapter 3: THE STAGES OF LIFE ACCORDING TO THE APOSTLE JOHN

> I am writing to you, little children,
> > because your sins have been forgiven
> > > on account of his name.
>
> I am writing to you, fathers,
> > because you have known the one who
> > > has existed from the beginning.
>
> I am writing to you, young people,
> > because you have overcome the evil one.
>
> I have written to you, little children,
> > because you have known the Father.
>
> I have written to you, fathers,
> > because you have known the one who
> > > has existed from the beginning.
>
> I have written to you, young people,
> > because you are strong
> and because God's word remains in you
> > and you have overcome the evil one.

—1 John 2:12-14 (ISV)

First John 2:12-14 is a wonderful picture of the three basic stages of life. Caught up in his theme, the apostle John breaks out into beautiful poetry. There are two stanzas, each characterized by a pattern of three. Verses 12-13b contain three statements beginning with "I am writing to you...," while verses 13c-14 repeat the pattern in a different tense, "I have written to you...." In both stanzas three groups are mentioned: little children, fathers, young people.

This threefold grouping relates to spiritual maturity, not necessarily to years as reckoned by the calendar (though spiritual maturity and natural age often coincide). John is writing to faithful members of his church who have not been led astray by those who have gone out from them. He writes to assure them in the face of opposition that they indeed have been forgiven, have known the Father, and have overcome the evil one (Satan). For John, it was of supreme importance that Christians should remember the benefits they have in Christ, for these would be their best defense against sin and error.

Although the sequence "little children—fathers—young people" does not fit a strictly chronological scheme, these terms do seem to denote three types of Christians. In the Body of Christ there are "little children" (those who are babies in Christ), "young people" (those who have grown in grace), and "fathers" (those who are spiritually mature, having fed for many years on the meat of God's Word). John's essential point is that there should be growth and progress in the life of every Christian.

Similarly, the author of Hebrews urges his readers to leave "the basic doctrines of Christ" and be carried along on to maturity (Hebrews 6:1)—not to throw away the first things, but to feed on the deeper things of God as we grow. Paul likewise writes, "So then, just as you received Christ Jesus the Lord, continue to live in him. For you have been rooted in him, and you are being built up and strengthened in the faith" (Colossians 2:6-7). Paul himself is a good example of one who had reached Christian maturity, and such is reached only by feeding on the Word of God.

Here in 1 John 2:12 we are told that all believers alike possess the initial blessing of the forgiveness of sins. From that point on, believers are to advance in spiritual growth and maturity. We should not always remain spiritual infants, but should grow into young manhood and fatherhood. Since these differences in maturity are true of any earthly family, let's take a closer look at these three family groups, the words addressed to each, and the relevance of John's poem to our task as parents.

The Words to the Little Children

To begin with, the readers are addressed as "little children." John uses two different Greek words to describe these believers: *teknia* (verse 12) and *paidia* (verse 13c). In the context, the word *teknia* has the sense of "born ones" or "offspring" and emphasizes the helplessness and immaturity of those in view, while the term *paidia* carries the notion of "children under instruction." To put it another way, *teknia* thinks of a child as young in age, and *paidia* thinks of a child as young in experience and thus in need of training and discipline. The *teknia*, we are told, have had their sins forgiven for Christ's sake. The *paidia*, on the other hand, have come to know to know the Father through instruction.

It is instructive to observe the Greek tenses used by John. "Have been forgiven" and "have known" both translate Greek perfect tenses, which emphasize a state that results from a completed action. That is to say, the readers' sins were forgiven at some time in the past and remain forgiven. Likewise, they have come to know God in his character as Father in a permanent, abiding sense. Forgiveness naturally comes first in the listing, for it is the foundational experience of the Christian life and the condition of fellowship with God. This forgiveness is based on the "name" of Christ. In Scripture, the name of a person stands for that person's character. Thus, to be forgiven "for his name's sake" is to be forgiven on the basis of who Christ is and what he has done for us. As long as the person and work of Christ endure, the believer's sins are forgiven!

Let us now apply this to parenting. As Christian parents, we too have obligations toward our "little children." As innocent children in a wicked world, they are in constant danger of being harmed by evil influences. Parents are to protect them from such dangers and remind them that their position in the family is absolutely secure, based on unconditional love. This complete, perfect, and permanent acceptance is based on our "name," that is, on our character as parents who are absolutely committed to raising our children in the nurture and admonition of the Lord. In addition to the complete security our children should experience, they should come to "know the Father." And just as the Holy Spirit indwells new-born believers and causes them to cry out, "Abba! Father!" (Galatians 4:6), so children look to their earthly father for guidance. In short, just as Christians have a Heavenly Father to care for their needs, so children need dads who will care for them.

New-born Christians not only have come to know God as their Father, but they know something *about* the Father as well. God deals with his children not only through *protection* but also through *instruction*. He nurtures and chastens his children for their spiritual good (Hebrews 12:7-11) so that they might bear much fruit for his glory (John 15:1). Likewise, parents need to instruct their children and at times even discipline them in order that they might bear the fruit of the Holy Spirit in their lives.

The little children, then, have made a good start by knowing that their sins have been forgiven and that God is their Father, and with proper guidance they may advance from there. In a sense, every believer remains a child in God's family, no matter how mature he or she may have become spiritually. We always need the Father's provision, and we always bask in the sunshine of his unconditional love. But because of the constant danger of spiritual seduction, we are to grow up into "young people" and into "fathers."

The Words to the Young People

The expression "young people" speaks of those who are growing up but who are not yet spiritually mature. It is they who receive special attention in John's poem, as is indicated by their being placed last in each stanza.

These young people are believers in conflict. They have three implacable enemies: the world, the flesh, and the devil. Although every believer is engaged in spiritual warfare, young adults are especially susceptible to the tests and trials of life. Young adulthood can be a turbulent time! Young people have reached a stage of spiritual development where they are expected to bear the heat of the attack, whether that attack is an overt one or a subtle undermining of faith. This very conflict brings them continually into contact with the powers of darkness, and thus they are in peculiar danger.

Notice what John says about the young people. First of all, they have overcome the evil one (verse 13b). They have defeated Satan and his hosts. Thus, assurance of victory is the primary characteristic of young believers. Moreover, although the world lies under the power of the evil one, the young men "are strong." John explains the basis of their strength: they have the Word of God abiding in them. Like Christ who overcame Satan in the wilderness through the Word of God abiding in him ("It is written!" was his weapon), so his people prevail against their spiritual foe with "the sword of the Spirit, which is the word of God" (Ephesians 6:16). For both Christ and Christians, the Word is uniquely able to convey not only knowledge of the truth, but also final deliverance from the power of evil.

John's words of assurance to the young men have tremendous relevance to parents. Since Satan still owns the world and runs it, young people are in a very dangerous place. They are like soldiers deep in the enemy's territory. Their only safety lies in keeping in touch with their Commander in glory. If they are to know victory over the enemy, they must be able to say, as Christ did, "It is written!", "It is written!", "It is written!" They must spend time in God's Word to know the One who gives them victory. May I say plainly that it is not possible for young people to live the Christian life without a knowledge of God's Word. Only as the Scriptures abide in them can they have spiritual power and courage. Only as they feed on meat of the Word can they have convictions and not be tossed about by every wind of doctrine. Only as they drink of the water of life can they have a real purpose in living. We parents, too, can be strong when we use the only offensive weapon God has given us—the Word of God abiding in us.

The Words to the Fathers

The senior believers, as is stated twice, "have known the one who has existed from the beginning." This is the same God as the little children have come to know as the Father, but the fathers, through long experience, have come to know God in a fuller and deeper sense. Over the years they have sought, and have been granted, such intimacy with God that he knows them, as he knew Moses, "face to face" (Deuteronomy 34:10).

Fathers in spiritual growth have reached the stage where God fills their vision. Nothing is added to this, because there can be nothing beyond knowing him. Paul speaks of this same wondrous intimacy when he says, "I want to know Christ" (Philippians 3:10). All who share Paul's passion are truly fathers in Christ. Through reading and meditation on the Word, they are brought into close, personal fellowship with Christ. They are "fathers," for they will produce spiritual children—the fruit of their Christian life, character, and testimony.

Such a personal, intimate knowledge of Christ is a humbling experience. Knowing God always leads to a deep sense of one's own unworthiness in the light of his grace and glory. At the beginning of his ministry, Paul could say that he was "the least of the apostles" (1 Corinthians 15:9). Later he could claim that he was "the very least of all the saints" (Ephesians 3:8). Near the end of his life, however, he could admit to being the chief of sinners (1 Timothy 1:15), since the knowledge of Christ always leads to humility and more humility. There is thus a vast difference between knowing truths about God and knowing *him*. When John speaks about the increasing knowledge of God, he does not mean that the Christian would become more and more of a learned theologian. He means that the Christian can become more and more intimate with God as lover and friend. Knowing the truth easily leads to pride; knowing God is the fruit of the soul fully occupied with him. Jesus himself faced the temptation of pride at the age of thirty. Satan used the lust of the flesh and of the eyes, and the pride of life, to try and defeat the Savior. Jesus resisted the devil by resting in the love of the Father and in his intimate knowledge and enjoyment of God.

What, then, is Christian "fatherhood"? It involves nothing less than a radical decision to put God first in every area of one's life. The world has ten thousand appeals. It has something to suit every disposition, every type of person. The Christian may use many of these things, but never abuse them. The moment anything comes between the soul and God, it is "not from the Father, but is from the world" (1 John 2:16).

Saying "no," however, often means saying "yes" to something higher. If "fathers" do not love the world, it is because a deeper, sweeter, greater love has been shed abroad in their hearts—the love of God. While it is to be hoped that all the children of God experience such love, there are some men and women whom we naturally describe as people who "know God" because over the years they have drunk deeply at the fountain of Christ. This is what the British author Malcolm Muggeridge described when he wrote:

> I may, I suppose, regard myself or pass for being a relatively successful man. People occasionally stare at me in the streets—that's fame. I can fairly easily earn enough to qualify for admission to the higher slopes of the Internal Revenue—that's success. Furnished with money and a little fame even the elderly, if they care to, may partake of trendy diversions—that's pleasure. It might happen once in a while that something I said or wrote was sufficiently heeded for me to persuade myself that it represented a serious impact on our time—that's fulfillment. Yet I say to you—and I beg you to believe me—multiply these tiny triumphs by a million, add them all together, and they are nothing—less than nothing, a positive impediment—measured against one draught of that living water Christ offers to the spiritually thirsty, irrespective of who or what they are.[11]

Such knowledge of Christ is the acme of Christian joy and glory. The "fathers" guarantee the possibility of such knowl-

---

[11]David Porter, *The Practical Christianity of Malcolm Muggeridge* (Downers Grove, IL: IVP, 1983) p. 5.

edge, and it is available to the "little children" and "young men" of each new generation of Christians.

Guideposts on the Road to Maturity

Let me now be more specific about the relevance of John's threefold description of human development and its relevance to the task of parenting. As Christian parents, we are obligated to guide our children through these stages of life. But how? Try these suggestions in your family to promote the proper climate for growth:

1. *Provide your "little children" with a secure world in which they come to know God's unconditional love.*

Secure relationships in the home are the primary environment for raising secure adults. Some specific ways to provide these relationships for your children include:

Love your spouse. The relationship between a husband and a wife is the foundation on which children build their sense of security. A child's greatest desire is that his or her parents love each other and thus model godly love and fidelity. Dads and moms need to covenant before God to remain married, to love each other selflessly, and to allow the love of God to permeate their home. The fidelity of our love for one another will transfer to our children, who will, by our example, learn to exhibit fidelity in everything they do. Children need to know that they are loved by both parents and feel the security that parental love provides in an unlovely world.

Of course, strong marriages take effort on the part of both spouses. Separation and divorce can be avoided only if both work hard to make the marriage succeed. This does not mean that parents can never disagree, but when they do it must be made clear to the children that separation and divorce is not an option.

Practice quantity time and not just quality time. We cannot simply devote a few "quality" moments a week to the nurturing of our children. Many parents, including pastors and Christian leaders, have sacrificed their families on the altar of service to God. Children need *time.* They need for us to share in their world and in their interests. The key is our willingness to engage our children where they are in terms of their development. Significant quality time occurs when our children are caught up in an experience that communicates caring. Play is the language of children, and we speak their language when we participate with them in their world. The resulting bonding, unity, and identity give a family a uniqueness that says, "We are here for each other."

Treat your children as children, not as miniature or immature adults. A child thinks differently from an adult. Consequently, the adult who expects a child to possess developed mental processes is apt to be very frustrated and, in turn, to make life miserable for the child. Lack of intelligence is not the issue; children are simply locked into a different viewpoint. Younger children are limited to seeing a moral world in self-centered terms. The day will come when the child understands the difference between right and wrong. On the other hand, it is never too early to engage a child in simple reasoning about right and wrong. Family members need mutual respect and a shared concern for righteousness. Rewards and punishments have their place, but use them sparingly, with consistency, and with gentle kindness, or they will lose their effectiveness.

Beware of the pressure of achievement. As parents, we are not given children to meet *our* needs of status or vicarious success. Yet all too often we are driven by the fear of not attaining "perfect" parenthood. "Hey, my kid is ten, and he's not mastered the violin, and he hasn't been in the Little League World Series, and he hasn't even been to Space Camp, for goodness' sake." Our children don't need to find their worth in their performance. We need to let them know that God has made them with unique capabilities, then encourage and support them to be all that they can be.

Remember, too, that God does not intend for us to grovel in guilt for matters beyond our control. The emphasis of parenting is on competence, not in perfecting a son's or daughter's behavior. Wise parents accept imperfections, improve the ones that are correctable, and find ways to compensate for those that are not. And, by so doing, they teach their children to do the same.

Help them to "know the Father." The warm circle of the family is still the habitat in which God intends for children to come to know him personally. Children are free to choose, to believe or not to believe, but parents can encourage them to accept the Christian faith as their own. The way God showed his love toward us—reaching out to us while we were still sinners—is the way faith can be shared with children.

As parents we can do things that cultivate an atmosphere of Godliness in our homes. We can pray together spontaneously—giving thanks for a sunset, asking God's help on a math test, praying for a safe vacation. We can speak often of God's love and care, letting our children know that the joy we experience as a family is a gift from God. We also need to show our children that the Lord longs to welcome them into his family. "Let the little children come to me," Jesus said, "and stop preventing them. For the kingdom of heaven belongs to people like these" (Matthew 19:14). Through our prayers and guidance, we can play an important role in seeing God's saving work in our children's lives.

Give them the foundation of God's Word. A final important way to shape our children's lives is by teaching them the stories and words of the Bible. Scripture memorization and Bible reading are essential elements in this process. But relating Scripture to real life is the best way of teaching the Bible, assuming that we know the Word ourselves and can draw from its resources. For example, when my wife was working with our sons to plant our vegetable garden, she often referred to the Lord's words about harvesting the kind of seeds we plant.

God's Word must also be woven into the negative experiences of life. The Bible teaches that God uses difficulties to bring us to spiritual maturity, and how parents face tough times teaches children a great deal. If children see no difference between the way their Christian parents handle difficulties and the way unbelieving parents handle similar situations, they will have every reason to question their parents' faith. But when the Word of God is woven into the fabric of our own lives as parents first, our children will learn that the Bible is more than a rabbit's foot to bring us good luck.

2. *Nurture the "young people" in your family in their faith, personal identity, and ability to live responsibly in the world.*

As children become young adults, the role of the family in their life changes. For preschool children, family is the only world they know. Their world grows during their elementary school years as teachers and classmates take some of the time that used to be spent with family. By junior high school, the family has changed from being the center of the individual's existence to being one of many arenas in which life is shared. The family's role changes from a single emphasis (providing a secure environment for a dependent child) to a double emphasis (accommodating a youth's continuing dependency needs while nurturing the youth in a growing sense of independence). A few ways to accomplish this include:

Communicate that you believe in your teens. The apostle John had nothing but praise for the "young people" among his readers. Young people are greatly encouraged by an adult who sees beyond the outward appearance to the real inner person. As parents we need to affirm our confidence in our teens' unique talents and in their ability to make a lasting contribution to their family, church, and world because of who God has made them to be. Parents who are able to affirm good behavior and reward good intentions, yet understand failures and offer forgiveness, will have children who will trust them and follow their advice.

One important way of showing our teens that we believe in them is by doing things with them. The crucial thing is that it be the teen who decides what to do. A few years ago my oldest son Nathan wanted to join a train club. He asked me if he could begin attending the club's weekly meetings, which meant a long drive on my part. We decided to go. Nathan is now a valued member of the club, and I have learned along with him the whole fascinating world of building and operating a model railroad.

In short, trust is a necessity of life for teenagers. Without parental trust, young people have little chance of developing self-esteem and a confident sense of their own identity.

When youth feel parents don't trust them, destructive behavior is often the result.[12]

Provide boundaries that are consistent with biblical principles. John says that young people can be strong if the Word of God abides in them. I heartily agree. I don't accept the fact that rebellion is an inevitable part of growing up. Youth don't need to act moody, or be cynical, or drop out to be healthy. Parents do not help teenagers when they brush aside unacceptable behavior and say, "Well, they're just being kids." The parenting task demands that we set up guidelines for our teens and make sure they understand what happens if they overstep the established bounds.

These boundaries should be based on the principles found in Scripture, remembering that our ultimate goal in parenting is not only to keep our teens from engaging in sinful behavior, but also to cultivate a transformed mind whereby they learn to evaluate behavior and attitudes in light of God's truth and grace. Teenagers are moving into a stage of intellectual maturity in which they can begin to tackle some of the great issues of life. During this period of searching and questioning, the Bible stands as the only sure, authoritative word on matters of faith and practice. Eventually, the faith of childhood must give way to a personalized, mature faith.

Provide them with significant adult relationships. Much has been written about the extent to which teens are influenced by their peers. However, while peers may be the most *immediate* influence on young people, adults are undoubtedly the most *important*. Teenagers need significant interaction

---

[12]See M. P. Strommen, *Five Cries of Youth* (New York: Harper & Row, 1974) p. 49. Interestingly, Strommen concluded that about 20% of teenagers surveyed lived a life of self-hatred.

with mature adults in order to become mature adults themselves. Young people may protest that "adults are *so* dumb," but when crises and heartbreaks come, most teens are anxious to seek the help of adults.

Secure relationships in the home are the primary source of significant adult relationships. Research reveals that the strongest influence on the life of a teenager is his or her parents. Parental influence decreases while peer influence increases each year through the ninth grade, but at no time does peer influence outweigh parental influence.[13] As our children get older we can share more and more insights from our own lives and relate the lessons we've learned from both good and bad experiences. Despite what some are saying, parents are still the essential value givers during this period. This responsibility should not be abdicated to the teen's peer group or youth pastor!

However, because teenagers require a growing independence from parents, they need other mature adults to turn to for advice, support, and godly examples. This is what Solomon meant when he advised, "Do not forsake... the friend of your father" (Proverbs 27:10). Even children who have good relationships with their parents still need guides and encouragers. Youth pastors, teachers, coaches, and family friends provide the essential complimentary components for a secure adult world in which young people can learn what it means to be a Christian adult.

In establishing such relationships, it is vital that parents and youth leaders not give in to the temptation to stop being adults in order to relate better with youth. An adult orientation is necessary so that teens know whom to approach

---

[13]See P. Benson, D. Williams, and A. Johnson, *The Quicksilver Years* (San Francisco: Harper & Row, 1987) pp. 27-30. This influence was tested over six topics: trouble in school; how to handle feelings, drugs, and alcohol; questions about sex; feelings of guilt; and deciding what to do with one's life.

when spiritual crises or moral values need to be discussed. Adults need to accept their role as models and guides, and should try to be available to youth when they ask for help.

Develop an atmosphere of freedom to explore ideas without ridicule. Most young people are smart enough to realize that there aren't answers to every question in life. What they are concerned about is how to cope with life's contradictions. They need to know that mom and dad will respect their opinions and not put them on trial for questioning their parents' beliefs and values. One of the most important steps in developing strength in young people is to teach them how to express themselves clearly, to be able to think through unanswered questions, and to be able to defend their opinions while respecting those who have different ones.

If parents can learn to be open to their teenager's tentative ideas, the teenager will be more willing to talk, and parents will have a better chance to influence the belief system their teens are formulating. On the other hand, teens are deeply hurt by parents who have no time to listen to them. Nothing softens the heart of a young person as quickly as honest expressions of affirmation such as, "I love you and want to understand you" or "It really matters to me what you are thinking." In the course of writing this book, I'd often ask my sons, "If I were to say this to a group of young people, what do you think they would say to me?" This gave them an opportunity to tell me their opinion of what other children think, which, of course, really gave me insight into what *they* were thinking. Conversations about values, ideals, and problems are a marvelous adventure. Be sure you don't miss it.

3. *Show your family what true "fatherhood" involves. Spiritual fatherhood is the capacity to enjoy a unique intimacy with God.*

Children need their parents to be their primary role models of a healthy relationship with God. Being good role models doesn't mean being perfect. Nevertheless, there are concrete ways parents can improve the roles they model and provide for their children.

Be aware of your influence. Parents who keep active in their minds that they are modeling for their children how to live will find it easier to evaluate the messages they are sending. Influence is the capacity to affect the thinking or actions of another person without force or authority. Young adults will be influenced to a greater or lesser degree by every person they come in contact with. The power of influence will occasionally even determine life's direction for a young person. So determine to be a good influence, and pray for others to influence your youth in godly ways. Of course, you may do everything "right" as parents and your children still not become the kind of persons you want them to be. Remember that teenagers are adults and can make choices on their own. The example you set can only help steer them in the right direction, not ensure that they become responsible adults. Ultimately you must give your children to God and pray for them constantly.

Practice now the values you want to see in your children someday. Children hear what is practiced more than what is preached. As Jesus walked with his disciples, he taught them. That's what parenting is all about. We don't just talk, we integrate talk with life. Let's not expect our children to excel in areas that we don't value ourselves. Of course, I'm not talking about a sinless life, but rather a life consumed with God, a life touched by his grace and empowered by his Spirit. Children need parental role models who are courageous enough to let God be the only all-sufficient one.

Pray with and for your children. When we go to the Lord with our children, they learn to look to God and not to us for guidance. When we pray with our children, we are weaning them from reliance on parents who will not always be with them to dependence upon the God who will never leave them nor forsake them. In praying with our children, their focus shifts from themselves to God, and their strength to face their daily trials is renewed. Parent, are you praying with intense faith for your children? Do you truly believe that God will answer your prayers? The alternative is to work yourself into a frenzy of worry.

My hope in making these suggestions is that they will help families to talk together about the value choices they make daily and, beyond talking, to find ways to act. In terms of your awareness of your own family, which of these need more attention? Parents must seek creative ways to address the challenge of development facing their children today.

Jesus himself provides the best model for relating to people at their levels of understanding. As he taught the twelve, he gradually revealed more and more of himself as their understanding developed. He delegated responsibilities and involved his disciples in ministry, not all at once, but as they were prepared and willing to accept the tasks. Finally, Jesus ascended into heaven and left his followers to carry out the Great Commission. He shows us the necessity—and wisdom—of teaching our children at their own level of development.

Part Two:

Parenting Principles from the Life of Jesus

Chapter 4: THE HOME TRAINING OF JESUS

The child continued to grow and to become strong.
He was filled with wisdom, and God's favor was
with him. —Luke 2:40 (ISV)

J esus is the great misunderstood Person of history. Three recent books on Jesus (all published in 1992) are a case in point.

Barbara Thiering, an Australian scholar, in her book *Jesus the Man: A New Interpretation from the Dead Sea Scrolls*, presents quite a startling picture of Jesus. She suggests that Jesus had been married, had fathered three children, had then divorced and remarried.

Shortly afterward, the British journalist A. N. Wilson published a book entitled simply *Jesus*. This book documents Wilson's much-publicized rejection of religion in general and of Christianity in particular.

A third book was by John Spong, the well-known Bishop of Newark, New Jersey. In *Born of a Woman*, Spong claims that the Virgin Birth has largely been responsible for the oppression of women.

This "interest" in the historical Jesus has reached the level of tabloid journalism! Yet the real, historical Jesus still has some surprises for us. What did it mean to be a first-century Jewish child, and what can that teach us about parenting?

Nurturing Your Children at Home

To begin with, Jewish education emphasized the teaching of children in the home. Children were a great joy and reward (Psalm 127:3-5). Education at home began soon after a child could talk, and certainly by the age of three. Parents taught prayers and songs that children learned by repetition, just as children today learn nursery rhymes. This priority given to home education stemmed from the value of children in Jewish society.

Parental responsibility for education was clearly defined. A father was expected to give his son instruction in religion and in the history of the Jewish people. Every other activity, even eating, gave place to this paramount duty. He was also required to teach his son a trade (often his own), since a boy without a trade was thought to have been trained for life as a thief. A father's other responsibilities included finding his son a wife and teaching him how to swim.

The Jewish mother played a considerable role in a child's education, particularly in the earliest years. The Rabbis were fond of saying that knowledge of the Law was to be found in those who sucked it at their mother's breast. A mother was expected to assist in teaching her sons, but her major responsibility was to train her daughters to be successful homemakers. Girls learned the skills of cooking, weaving, sewing, caring for children, and grinding grain. At times they helped with the harvest or were expected to help guard the vineyard and family flock.

At home, children early became aware of their religious heritage. They learned their own "history"—that of their tribe, clan, and family. Long before they could go to synagogue, prayers and family rituals, whether of the weekly Sabbath or of the annual Feasts, were indelibly impressed on their minds. Children were encouraged to ask questions about the meaning of religious symbols such as the Passover ritual (Exodus 12:26). Children undoubtedly had questions about objects they encountered, whether sacred vessels, ornaments, or clothing used in tabernacle or temple worship.

Education consisted of learning the Law through listening and oral repetition, along with the study of the written text. Students were expected to master their studies, preparing themselves to take responsibility for obeying the Law as adults. Teaching often came in the form of proverbs or parables, devices often used by Jesus (cf. Mark 4:1-2). An open sharing of knowledge occurred in "question and answer" periods.

Since the ancient Hebrews were generally regarded as the most proficient musicians in the Near East, it is probable that basic instruction in singing and playing instruments was received at home.

It was in such circumstances, and under such influences, that the early years of Jesus passed. He could read and expound the Scriptures and was knowledgeable enough to discuss theology with the learned men in the temple. In studying with his parents he received the elementary education common to most Jewish boys at that period. The home was the setting for education, and the "creed" to be recited was no series of abstract truths but the "old, old story" of the events that brought salvation.

Notice how Luke summarizes Jesus' life between infancy and age twelve:

> After doing everything required by the Law of the Lord, Joseph and Mary returned to their hometown of Nazareth in Galilee. The child continued to grow and to become strong. He was filled with wisdom, and God's favor was with him. —Luke 2:39-40

Here we learn several things about Jesus' childhood:

- Jesus was given every opportunity to "grow and become strong." His home environment provided a healthy incubator for physical, emotional, and spiritual growth. Joseph and Mary themselves provided this opportunity, performing everything "according to the Law of the Lord." *They were meticulous about how they raised their son.*

- Jesus' growth was a very normal, natural process. There was no force, no pushing on the part of Jesus' parents. They weren't anxious to get their gifted young son before the public. He was allowed to develop at a normal pace.

- Jesus' *spiritual* life developed—"God's favor was with him." In fact, in Jewish thought, the highest goal of life is "the knowledge of God" (*daät elohim*). All education was directed toward this end. This concept differed drastically from the Greek idea of education, where "know yourself" (*gnothi seauton*) was the central goal.

At least three implications concerning parenting are found in this passage. The first is the importance of childhood training in the "wisdom" of the Scriptures. As Jesus grew, he could rest on the absolutes he learned as a child. Children profit immensely by specific biblical instruction in the home. They also need to derive spiritual strength and guidance from individual, personal Bible study. Personal Bible study aids children in making direct applications of biblical insights to their own life. However, parental guidance and instruction are still needed. The danger is that the child will make farfetched or overly subjective applications that distort the basic biblical message. Children also need a clear and systematic presentation of the contents of the Scriptures. They need an overview of what kind of book the Bible is and what its central themes are. Such commonplace terms as "prophet," "apostle," and "justification" need to be defined in such a way that children can understand them.

Jesus undoubtedly committed Scripture to memory. Likewise, children today need to learn as much Scripture as they can at an age when their memories are more able and retentive. Previously learned material will serve as a basis for later experience even if the material learned is not fully understood. Because of the numerous Bible translations available, memorizing Scripture is more complicated today than it was formerly. In my view, Scripture memorization can be done effectively only from one version or translation. I would recommend the use of the International Standard Version New Testament with CD-ROM (ISBN 1891833111), the International Standard Version Bible with CD-ROM (ISBN 1891833138) or the International Standard Version Study Bible with CD-ROM (ISBN 1891833146), all published by Davidson Press, Inc.

Second, it is primarily the *parents'* job to convey biblical knowledge. Jesus' parents did. Timothy's parents did (2 Timothy 3:14). Perhaps your own parents did. From that knowledge you developed certain abiding principles of life. Following that process came wisdom—the ability to apply biblical principles to everyday life.

The formal content of what should be taught to a child is rightly determined by the parents. Of course, parents need to phrase that content in life-related ways that children can understand. This task will require dedicated and well-informed parents. The religious education of children needs to be a top priority of every parent. Religious education, like all education, involves listening to children as much as talking with them. Above all, it involves what our text calls "wisdom," that is, application to life in such a way that God's gift of physical life is completed and enriched by God's gift of eternal and abundant life. Many of our chil-

51

dren will spend a great deal of time later on in formal Christian education. Some will attend Christian colleges and seminaries. The foundation of religious education at home will prepare them for other areas of education and for responsible decision making.

Third, "doing everything required by the Law of the Lord" involved participation in the worship of God. Expression in worship is any attitude or action that brings to consciousness an awareness of God's presence. Children need time of both public and private worship. They draw from corporate worship the experiences and attitudes they need as worshiping persons. Wonder and awe are particularly present in childhood, and these dimensions of worship can be encouraged and enlarged with proper adult training. Children who wonder about God, who are curious and open to all areas of life, and who are open with their thoughts about God are worshiping. Worship can happen at church or at home, at school, and at play. When my son Matthew was four years old, we happened to be waiting for a green light when he asked, "How does God make the traffic lights change color?" His wonder was majestic, even though his deduction was wrong. The curiosity of a child is a gateway to great worship possibilities.

Before Jesus became a teacher of God's truth, he was allowed to grow, to become strong, to be filled with wisdom, to experience God's grace. That was the result of proper home training.

Is your home doing that?

Dads Are Teachers Too

Now a special word to dads (myself included). As we have seen, the Bible places fathers under the obligation of religious instruction for our children. God has called fathers to guide them into maturity, into the full potential he intends for them. Leadership in a family hinges on the father, with the wife complementing her husband's role.

When I give this teaching in churches, I am often asked, "But in Bible times weren't there schools to assist those fathers who were not in a position to meet this obligation personally?" The answer is yes and no. According to Rabbinical tradition, synagogue schools were established by Simeon ben Shetah under Salome Alexandra (76-67 B.C.). However, schools for boys did not become the general norm until the middle of the second century A.D.[14] Therefore, it is highly unlikely that the elementary school played a significant role in the education of children during Jesus' lifetime. His education at home was supplemented by sermons and lectures in the synagogue on the Sabbath, but his primary teacher was his father Joseph.

Think of the responsibilities a father shouldered back then. He was volunteering to perform at least seven functions to PREPARE his child:[15]

- *Production.* He would make the furniture, the clothing, and maybe even the house. Now that's all been taken over by industry.

- *Religion.* This has been transferred to the church or ignored altogether.

- *Education.* The schools have assumed this one.

- *Protection.* This function is now the responsibility of the police.

---

[14]See H. L. Strack and G. Steinberger, *Introduction to the Talmud and Midrash* (Minneapolis: Fortress, 1992) pp. 10-11.

[15]Adapted from A. Ortlund, *Building a Great Marriage* (Old Tappen, NJ: Revell, 1985) pp. 28-29.

- *Affection.* This involves nurture and child rearing, and is about the only function left delegated entirely to the home.

- *Recreation.* This has been taken over by TV, movies, and public functions.

- *Edification.* California's infamous self-esteem courses base self-esteem on humanism rather than Scripture.

No wonder men today feel they have less status and challenge in life! No wonder they pour themselves into their work, looking for something to challenge their male longing for importance and purpose!

What does the Bible say a dad should do? Here's the father's calling according to Deuteronomy 6:4-7:

> Hear, O Israel! The Lord our God is one Lord! And you shall love the Lord your God with all your heart and with all your soul and with all your might. And these words that I am commanding you this day shall be on your heart. You shall teach them diligently to your sons and shall talk of them when you sit in your house, when you walk, by the way when you lie down, and when you rise up.

Clearly, God intends fathers to have a unique role in the home. They are to lead their homes and be leaders in their churches.

What does such a leader look like? Is he tough like Clint Eastwood, tender like Jimmy Carter, funny like Bob Sackett, strong-willed like General Patton? Is he action-oriented like Peter, meek like Moses, quiet like John, bold like Paul? What is a real man like?

The biblical answer to these questions may be summed up in one word. A real man is a *godly* man. In the list of character qualities required of church leaders in 1 Timothy 3 and Titus 1, Paul gives us a balanced description of a godly leader. He is:

- Without blame, above reproach. No one is able to point a finger at him and say, "You did this or that and didn't make it right."

- Respectable, possessing dignity, and has a good reputation.

- Calm-tempered, patient, peaceable, not quick-tempered or easily angered, but gentle and considerate.

- Self-controlled, leading an orderly and disciplined life.

- Wise, sensible, and prudent.

- Just and fair-minded.

- Devout, holy, upright, well-behaved.

- Not contentious, argumentative, quarrelsome, or combative.

- Hospitable, friendly to all.

- Not selfish, self-willed, proud, or arrogant.

- Not a lover of money, not focused on things.

- A faithful husband, wise and careful in his relationships with the opposite sex.

- Capable and qualified to teach and to exhort in sound doctrine, able to show the error of false teaching.

- A good manager of his own household.

- Not a misuser of alcohol.

These are the qualities we dads should seek to develop in our own lives first and then in the lives of our children. Our mission is to help our children recognize the voice of God and respond appropriately, keeping in mind that the most effective teaching method is not lecturing but interaction. Communication is more like ketchup than milk. You've got to wait, prod a little, and wait some more. It's very important for parents to use and savor those "teachable moments" when children let down their guard and bring up subjects they would never feel comfortable discussing in a formal setting. It is through the endless daily small-talk ("when you sit in your home...") that we shape our children's outlook.

Our household is incredibly vocal. I end up talking to my sons about practically everything. It's easy to view such continual "trivial" conversations as interruptions. But from God's perspective they are opportunities to teach about: how big God is; the significance of the church; how to honor our spiritual leaders; how to trust the Lord; the importance of obedience; how to seek life's answers in God's Word; how to demonstrate love and compassion to others; and a million other truths.

Teaching our children is more than "lectures" or "daily devotions." We must teach *and* show. No church, no Sunday School, no Bible camp, no Christian school, no youth group can do the job that is left up to us. *We* are to teach and lead; *our* life will establish the direction for our children to follow.

Dad, your child's most important teacher is you! Your children need a father to embrace. They long for his tender affection, loving touch, and encouraging words. There is something deep inside of all children that craves the love of a father. It sensitizes even the most callous skin. It warms the coldest spirit. It softens the hardest heart. Your children crave this kind of love from their daddy.

A Father's Pledge

On the opposite page is a declaration of commitment to be a hands-on father. Read it aloud to God, sign it, and then put it in a safe place. Review it whenever necessary.

A FATHER'S PLEDGE

"I will positively influence the quality of my family life."

"I will love my wife as Christ loved the church and gave himself for her."

"I will not provoke my children to anger but will bring them up in the nurture and admonition of the Lord."

"I will receive the Word into my heart daily and will teach it diligently to my children."

"I will tenaciously retain the right to determine what will influence my children."

"I will learn to distinguish between healthy and unhealthy influences."

"I will set the pace spiritually as well as emotionally."

"I will not only cope with the present but also work toward the future."

"I will set long-range goals for my children."

"I will always ask, 'Does this contribute toward or detract from the characteristics I am trying to build into my children?'"

"I will consistently communicate acceptance and approval to my children."

"I will raise my children with the basic premise that certain things are right and other things are wrong."

"I will build rewards and security within the limits I set, and give discipline when the limits are exceeded."

"I will consistently enforce respect for and obedience to authority."

"I will never become too busy 'serving the Lord' to build love and godliness into the lives of my children."

Signed:_____

Date:_____

Chapter 5: JESUS AND THE AGE TWELVE TRANSITION

When he was twelve years old, they went up to the festival as usual. —Luke 2:42 (ISV)

Expecting Teenagers to Behave Like Adults

The early church apparently had little interest in the life of Jesus before his emergence as a teacher. There is something awe-inspiring in the grand silence that accompanies the thirty years before Jesus' birth and baptism. Only once is the silence broken in an incident recorded in Luke 2:41-52. *How important, then, is this event!* Since Scripture is given for our edification, I'm convinced the heavenly Parent cited this biblical example to help us with our own children and to show his understanding of his own creation.

(Incidentally, the simplicity of Luke's account contrasts with the often grotesque reports of Jesus as an exhibitionist and "boy wonder" in later non-canonical writings such as the Apocrypha. In the Gospel of Thomas, for example, Jesus rudely silences the teachers and becomes their instructor.)

Christian art has often portrayed this incident as "Jesus Teaching in the Temple." But a better title would be "Jesus Learning in the Temple." The young man of twelve did not go into the temple to lay down the Law. He went with simplicity of spirit and with an eager and teachable mind to learn from the Jewish elders. He was "listening to them and asking them questions." His instinctive attitude was that of respect for their authority. It was a mark of his divine Sonship that he could be so free from complacency, so eager for truth, so desirous to learn!

What is the significance of this account? At the age of twelve, Jesus would be beginning to make the transition into adult responsibility under the Law. Jewish sources differ with respect to the exact age when a boy became a *bar mitzvah* (son of the commandment), that is, when he attained the age of maturity and responsibility with respect to the keeping of God's commandments. The prevailing opinion seems to have been that at age thirteen a boy should fully shoulder that responsibility.[16] However, in order to prepare him to do this wise parents would ease him into this responsibility at the age of twelve.[17] Thus, when Jesus became twelve years old, Joseph and Mary took him to Jerusalem in order to attend the Passover festival.

You remember what happened next. Thinking Jesus was in the caravan when they started home, they did not miss him until the end of the day. Returning to Jerusalem, they found him in the temple talking with the teachers there. Luke says:

> When his parents saw him, they were shocked. His mother ask him, "Son, why have you treated us like this? Your father and I have been worried sick looking for you." He said to them, "Why were you looking for me? Didn't you know that I had to be in my Father's house?" —Luke 2:48-49

This passage is saying more than that Jesus was a precocious child. Luke's point is that, while Jesus was soon to be a teenager, *he would never be an adolescent*. Like any other twelve-year-old in his culture, he would be an adult and be treated as one by everyone in town. That's what the *bar mitzvah* ritual was all about.

---

[16]Cf. Mishnah, *Aboth* 5:21; *Niddah* 5:6.
[17]Cf. Mishnah, *Yoma* 8:4.

Today, the *bar mitzvah* is one of the most significant events in Jewish society. It is viewed as a turning point, as "a period when young people are obligated to control their own desires, accept accountability for mature religious actions, and assume adult community responsibilities."[18] At one point in the ceremony the father says, "Blessed be he who has freed me from the responsibility for this child!" This declaration sometimes brings a chuckle from other parents who realize that considerable financial and emotional support will be necessary for several more years. Nevertheless, many parents have tears in their eyes as they realize their little boy is becoming an adult. And, standing straight and tall, the "son of the commandment" demonstrates to the congregation his proficiency in the traditions of the community and commitment to the Covenant. At the conclusion of the ceremony, the congregation often sings a hymn of dedication, and a reception is held in the social hall.[19]

The *bar mitzvah* is the milestone in a young man's life when he formally assumes personal moral and religious responsibility and accountability. Far from being a trite, meaningless ritual, it provides a stability point for the rest of life. In the Middle Ages it developed into a rite of passage second to none. This rite was extended to girls in the form of the *bat mitzvah* (daughter of the commandment) during the twentieth century.[20] According to Jewish sources, this transition from childhood to adulthood would continue by degrees for several years beyond the twelfth birthday.

Clearly, God delights in celebrating the time when children become adults. And he delights in parents who blend

---

[18]D. A. Rausch, *Building Bridges: Understanding Jews and Judaism* (Chicago: Moody, 1988) p. 74.

[19]Ibid., pp. 74-75.

[20]P. Sigal, *Judaism* (Grand Rapids: Eerdmans, 1988) p. 253.

loving words and caring actions into a meaningful ceremony designed to leave a lasting memory. Hurrah for Jesus'
bar mitzvah!

The *Bar Mitzvah* and Psychology

The Jewish *bar mitzvah* is more than a religious obser-
vance. One can also refer to it as the acknowledgment of the
onset of *moral readiness*. Moral readiness is the capacity of a
person to make moral judgments. Others prefer to speak of
this transition in terms of the *age of accountability*. Accountability has to do with when it is right to praise or blame
people for their actions, or to feel proud of, or guilty about,
our own actions. This is contrasted with involuntary acts
that take place under compulsion or owing to ignorance.[21]
Perhaps the closest biblical reference to the idea of accountability is Romans 14:12: "Therefore, each of us will have to
give an account to God." The word used for "account" here
is the same word used in John 1:1 to describe Jesus as God's
"Word"—his account or expression of himself. The term implies that people are capable of responding to God. This response may be acceptance or rejection. Since responsibility
is implied in the ability to respond, the actions of a person
confronted by the truth and deliberately refusing to accept
that truth bring him or her full responsibility. Since the full-
est revelation of truth is in Jesus Christ, the age of accountability is ultimately related to a person's ability to accept or
reject the truth of the gospel.[22]

It is instructive to note how the insights of developmental psychology and the insights of Jewish theology mesh
together in the areas of value and wholeness in the child.

---

[21]See J. Glover, *Responsibility* (London: Routledge & Kegan Paul, 1970) pp. 1-4.
[22]See W. L. Hendricks, "The Age of Accountability," in C. Ingle (ed.), *Children and
Conversion* (Nashville: Broadman, 1970) pp. 84-97.

One example is the work of the Swiss psychologist Jean Piaget, who identified two stages of moral reasoning. *Heteronomous morality* is based on unilateral respect for authority. At this stage the rules are external laws set forth by adults and because of this they are sacred. *Autonomous morality* is based on mutual respect and equality. Rules are now understood in the context of adult relationships and eventually can become internalized principles.[23] Piaget's theory corresponds exactly to the transition described above in the Jewish *bar mitzvah*. It suggests that a large part of a child's moral development consists in the transition from obeying external rules to a stage of greater autonomy, where obedience is no longer an unquestioned end in itself, but the rules instead themselves are subjected to criticism.

Another example is psychologist Erik Erickson's eight phases in the life cycle of a person. Every phase involves a crisis that can be resolved by achieving some particular competence. Failure to achieve a competence results in a sense of incompletion in that phase. Erickson's eight phases of life are:

1. Trust vs. mistrust (babies).
2. Autonomy vs. shame and doubt (young infants).
3. Initiation vs. guilt (younger children).
4. Industry vs. inferiority (older children).
5. Identity vs. role confusion (adolescents).
6. Intimacy vs. isolation (young adults).
7. Generativity vs. stagnation (middle adults).
8. Ego integrity vs. disgust and despair (older adults).

What is interesting to observe is that four of these stages occur in childhood, while the four additional stages occur in

---

[23]See Jean Piaget, *The Moral Judgment of the Child* (London: Routledge, 1932).

the teen and adult years. Erickson has shown that, to the extent people succeed in shedding the assumptions of childhood, they are transformed into growing, becoming adults.[24]

A final example is James Fowler's six stages of human faith.[25] Fowler is interested in faith as a way humans see themselves, others, and the ultimate values of life. He contends that there are predictable stages of faith development that closely parallel other stages of life. Fowler's six stages are:

1. Intuitive-Projective Faith (early childhood).
2. Mythical-Literal Faith (ages six to twelve).
3. Synthetic-Conventional Faith (ages twelve and beyond).
4. Individuative-Reflective Faith (early adulthood).
5. Conjunctive Faith (mid-life and beyond).
6. Universalizing Faith (mid-life and beyond).

Fowler's third stage, "synthetic-conventional," is the stage associated with twelve-year-olds. It begins when a person is able to reflect on his or her own thinking. It is synthetic in the sense that the person attempts to integrate beliefs and self-image. It is called conventional because it is concerned with the expectations of others. This stage of faith development almost perfectly describes the Jewish *bar mitzvah*.

If teenagers are adults, not children, in their faith devel-

---

[24]See Erik Erickson, *Childhood and Society* (New York: W. W. Norton & Co., 1950) pp. 247-273. It would be a mistake to regard either Piaget's or Erickson's theory of moral development—no matter how useful we may find them—as providing a complete picture: they make no mention of the role of conscience or conversion. Even so, the idea of movement from heteronomous to autonomous morality is extremely useful.

[25]See James W. Fowler, *Stages of Faith* (San Francisco: Harper & Row, 1981).

opment, they are also adults in the area of cognition.[26] About the time of puberty, the brain undergoes a change that enables young people not only to learn more, but learn differently. Teenagers develop the capacity to conceptualize, analyze, and speculate. They can do abstract thinking, formulate theories, and explore complex constructs. At age twelve, Jesus was such a developing thinker. The temple leaders had the good sense to take him seriously.

Earlier we saw how the apostle Paul described the differences between his childhood and adulthood. In the area of reasoning he went from being a child to being an adult. Educational authorities realize this. Courses that require abstract thinking, such as algebra and chemistry, are generally not offered until after puberty. To measure the intellect of adults, psychologists use a whole different approach than they use to measure the intellect of children. Clearly, teenagers today are able to make important decisions, just as they did for thousands of years before we told them they couldn't.

The *bar mitzvah*, then, is a key transition when young people learn to take responsibility for their own lives. Thus we may offer the following definition of maturity: *Who I am may be best understood as a function of what I am willing to take responsibility for.*

Maturity involves both *individuation* and *autonomy*. Individuation means becoming a whole person, becoming an individual. It represents an achievement and is the product of development. Autonomy is self-regulation—the ability to control and direct one's self from within, rather than from external authority. It is expressed in three areas of life: (1) an individual's capacity for independent survival (through productive work); (2) independent thinking (looking at the

---

[26]See Ronald Kotesky, *Understanding Adolescence* (Wheaton: Victor, 1987) pp. 27-28.

world through one's own eyes); and (3) independent judgment (honoring one's internal values).

Of course, no one is autonomous or self-sufficient in the ultimate sense. Autonomy does not mean that one lives on a desert island or should act as if one did. It is the process of learning how to move by our own efforts, to put food into our own mouths, to enter into contracts with others, to engage in productive work—in other words, learning how to be *self-responsible.*

Autonomy begins with the recognition that I am ultimately responsibility for my own existence: that no one else is here on earth to take care of me or fill my needs. Self-responsibility entails my willingness to be accountable for my choices, decisions, and behavior.

In summary, the *bar mitzvah* is a time when young adults become personally responsible for their relationship with God and other people. It is a time to begin developing individuation and autonomy in the life of your child. When parents prepare their children for decision making, when they give as much freedom and responsibility as their teens can handle, when they take a positive step that bolsters their children's confidence, they have done what they can to prepare them for adulthood.

Teenagers Are Terrific

Parents who are willing to demand responsible behavior from their children need not dread the teen years. Teenagers can be terrific human beings. They give themselves to some worthy project with such devotion and intensity that the whole family gets caught up in it. Talents blossom in ways that amaze and delight their parents. Responsibilities are carried out in the teen years that impress all who live with teenagers. Social life expands both personal and family horizons. Ability to withstand temptation is remarkable.

They bring proud tears to the eyes of parents when they carry through some difficult project with success. Everywhere today teenagers are demonstrating what wonderful persons they can be.

What a difference now that childhood has been cast off! Parents, as your children become teenagers, it is time to hold them with an open hand, letting them be free to grow and find themselves—standing by them as a base of security, being available for guidance and prayer, and, above all, setting a worthy example. This is the time when you and your teenagers can enjoy the fruits of freedom, with mutual respect and faith in one another.

Chapter 6:   JESUS AND THE AGE THIRTY TRANSITION

Jesus himself was about thirty years old when he began his ministry. —Luke 3:23 (ISV)

Jesus and the Age Thirty Transition

We dare not overlook this "aside" by Luke. The Bible was not given for our *information* but for our *transformation*.

To understand Jesus' ministry, we often focus (rightly) on the events that occurred just after he left his parental home: his baptism, temptation, and association with John the Baptist. However, we now realize (thanks to developmental psychology) that abrupt changes of the kind described here by Luke occur frequently in men's lives at around the age of thirty, for reasons that are inherent in the process of becoming a mature adult.

Now, many of us have heard about the so-called "Mid-Life Crisis," but few of us have an inkling about the Age Thirty Transition. I first became aware of it at the age of thirty-three, while studying in Israel. One day it struck me that I was living in Jerusalem at the exact same physical and psychological age that Jesus was when he died on the cross. This triggered a desire within me to study the "seasons of life" in greater detail.

What is this "Age Thirty Transition"? Listen to one psychologist:

> The Age Thirty Transition frequently begins with a vague uneasiness, a feeling that something is missing or wrong in one's life and that some change

is needed if the future is to be worthwhile. Initially the main questions deal with the life one has created: What parts must I give up or appreciably change? What is missing from it? Toward the end of the Age Thirty Transition the man's orientation is more toward the future—finding a new life direction and making new choices or strengthening his commitment to choices already made.[27]

As we saw in Chapter 1, the Age Thirty Transition is the end product of the novice adult phase (see Luke 2:41-52). A man is now a full-fledged adult, committing himself to a new life structure through which he will reach his goals and aspirations. The major developmental task at this stage is discovering "who I am in a unique sense." Backed by all his life experiences and all the tasks he has already accomplished, he raises anew the question of his unique identity with greater intensity.

What brings about the Age Thirty Transition? Nothing less than a dawning awareness of one's mortality—the awareness that life is short, and if what one hopes to accomplish in life is going to get done before it is too late, a start will have to be made soon!

This idea of a "dawning sense of one's mortality" came home to me several years ago on a family vacation to Hawaii (where I was born and raised). All my life I had been an avid surfer (the 366 days-a-year type!), and now I kept my surfboard in my mother's home in Hawaii. I had boasted to my sons long and loud about their daddy's surfing exploits at Pipeline and Sunset Beach, and now they thought this was their big chance to see him in action.

---

[27]D. Levinson, *The Seasons of a Man's Life* (New York: Ballantine, 1978) p. 71.

When we walked into my former bedroom, my sons saw my surfboard. Immediately one of them asked, "Dad, are we now gonna get to see you catch some really big ones?" "Are you kidding?," I blurted out. "A guy could get killed doing that!" The Age Thirty Transition was at work! As a young man of sixteen I didn't notice the dangers of big wave riding. So what if you lost your board and tumbled in the white water until your lungs ached for air. So what if you had to swim a half mile to retrieve your surfboard that had been taken out to sea by the riptide. So what if your arms and legs were cut open by the coral reefs. To a teen-ager, life is an open highway, and death is a millennium away. But as a grown-up of thirty-five I had better things to do with my life than to risk losing it by surfing the twenty-five footers at Sunset Beach!

Each of us, I suppose, stumbles upon the issue of mortality with a similar sense of surprise. Eventually all of us must confront the reality of our own death. And, somehow, we must learn to live with it. As Max Lucado puts it:

> What you set out to do you didn't. You set out to avoid the trap of suburbia; now you're making mortgage payments. You swore you'd never be a corporate puppet, but now your closet is full of gray flannels. You determined to leave a legacy, but all you've left so far is a trail of diapers and check stubs.... The plumber wishes he'd gone to medical school and the doctor wishes he were a plumber. The woman who works regrets the time she didn't spend with her kids and the stay-at-home mom wishes she had a career.[28]

---

[28]M. Lucado, *He Still Moves Stones* (Dallas: Word, 1993) pp. 74-75.

When I consider the brevity of life, I find myself think-ing of Psalm 90, that great song about God's eternity and human finitude:

> The years of our life are threescore and ten,
>   or even by reason of strength fourscore;
> yet their span is but toil and trouble;
>   they are soon gone and we fly away.
> So teach us to number our days
>   that we may get a heart of wisdom. —Psalm 90:10, 12

Yes, the seasons of life are short. There is much to be done before we are "cut off." However, proper management of life is offered to the person of faith.

My research has convinced me that there really is some-thing to this "Age Thirty Transition." Consider the follow-ing:

- In the Talmud, the stages of life from five to 100 are carefully outlined, and age thirty is specifically men-tioned as the time in life when "full strength is at-tained."

- At Qumran, a man was not considered eligible for leadership until he was thirty.

- In Israel, the age of fitness to serve in the temple was thirty.

- According to Genesis 41:46, Joseph was thirty years old when he was set over the land of Egypt.

- According to 2 Samuel 5:4, David was thirty years old when he became king of Israel.

- Ezekiel received his great prophecy in his thirtieth year (Ezekiel 1:1).

- From secular religious history, Confucius traces the stages of his life from fifteen to seventy, and says of his thirtieth year that it was then that he planted his feet "firmly upon the ground."

What, then, can we learn about Jesus—and us—from Luke's statement that Jesus was "about thirty" when he began his public ministry?

Let's begin by reviewing what Jesus was like at age thirty. He was his parent's first born son (Luke 2:7). Now, in the Jewish culture, being the first born son was a tremendous responsibility. It involved the care of any younger siblings. You were considered to be the chief heir to your father's wealth and were expected to take his place as the head of the family when he died.

My wife Becky is the eldest of six children in her family. She was raised in Ethiopia as a missionary kid. During her boarding school days, she was responsible to care for her siblings—making sure, for example, that they didn't fall down the hole when they went to the outhouse at night! I, on the other hand, am the youngest of four children. How opposite we are in our in terms of our outlook on life!

Not only was Jesus the eldest son, he was the eldest son in a relatively large Jewish family. His family included four younger brothers and at least two sisters (see Mark 3:31-35; 6:3). Moreover, like his father, Jesus was a carpenter (or, better, "builder"; Jesus was quite possibly part of a fairly lucrative middle class business operation). He and his brothers undoubtedly worked with their father in various building projects, many of which probably took place in the large Hellenized city of Sepphoris, located just a few miles from

Nazareth. As the eldest son, Jesus no doubt had special responsibilities in the family business.

It is clear that when Jesus began his public ministry, Joseph was dead by this time, since he is missing from all the accounts of this period. This means that at some time prior to his baptism in the Jordan River, Jesus became the head of his deceased father's family.

Now, the loss of a father by anyone at any time is difficult. But can you imagine the trauma of the loss of a father by an eldest son in a large Jewish family! From that moment on, it was Jesus' responsibility to shoulder his father's trade, for he was now the family's chief means of support. He would have to learn how to care for and manage these responsibilities in an efficient, competent manner. As time went on, his relation to his mother may have become problematical, for she undoubtedly began to lean more and more on her highly resourceful son. This would intensify sibling rivalries and perhaps be accompanied by other emotions in Jesus: anger at the premature loss of his father, fear about taking his place, anxiety over the future, and so forth.

It was precisely in such a situation, says Luke, that Jesus followed the crowds to the Jordan River and received baptism at the hands of John. At the height of his career as a builder, he apparently "shirked" all of his human responsibilities and went away to "do his own thing." The burden of caring for the family now fell on the shoulders of James, the next eldest son. Jesus' family simply couldn't understand how he could do this to them.

At this time, tensions began to develop between Jesus and his mother, brothers, and sisters. The Bible says that Jesus' brothers did not believe on him (John 7:5), and at one point in his ministry his family thought he was crazy and was determined to seize him and bring him back home (Mark 3:19-21). Later, Jesus distanced himself from them when he said, "Who are my mother and my brothers?" Then looking at the people sitting around him, he said, "Here are my mother and my brothers! Whoever does the will of God is my brother and sister and mother" (Mark 3:33-35).

Note carefully what had happened in Jesus' life. *Jesus' "Age Thirty Transition" was nothing less than a radical shift in loyalty from his human family to God's family, from earthly priorities to heavenly priorities, from the physical to the spiritual!* Think about it! Few situations in life are as demanding and emotionally complex as that of a son, caught up in assuming his father's role, shifting his loyalty to something else. But for Jesus, the spiritual was more important than the physical. His true family was the family of God, and his sole aim in life was to do the will of God, his heavenly Father.

As a catalyst to break away from his earthly family in order to fulfill his own unique destiny and mission, Jesus was baptized at the hands of John. This act meant a decisive break with his past and the beginning of a new ministry. By receiving baptism at the hands of John, he displayed his willingness to follow the will of God even if that meant risking alienation from his earthly family.

But God the Father was right there to affirm his Son. As soon as Jesus had come up out of the water, a voice from heaven confirmed that Jesus had made the right choice. In essence, the Father told Jesus, "You are *my* Son (not Mary's), whom I love very much. And what you just did made me very happy!" (Mark 1:11).

Immediately afterwards, Jesus wrestled with Satan over *how* he was to fulfill his unique role as the Son of God. During the temptations in the wilderness, he refused to follow Satan and instead submitted himself to the will of the Father.

Listen to me, dear parent. This is the divine Model our children need! Jesus, "the tempted" one, at the right time humbles himself in baptism, says no to grandiosity, and with God's help goes on to become everything he was meant to be.

The lesson? *I believe there is no greater thing we can do as parents than to give our children absolute freedom to be all that God wants them to be.* We need to help them to see that their main priority in life is finding the will of God, and then doing it with all their might. As a famous missionary put it before he died, "Wherever you are, *be all there*, and live to the hilt whatever you are convinced is the will of God for your life!"

Jesus, the central figure of our faith, went through such a transformation at his baptism. My personal faith is strengthened by this discovery. I discover that my Master entered so fully into my humanity that he subordinated all to the will of God. He models for me how to die to self and offers me encouraging companionship as I face my own mortality. Though I may be "miles away" from my own physical death, I can die daily from a different perspective.

At the end of his earthly life, Jesus said, "Father, I glorified you on earth by completing the task you gave me to do" (John 17:4). There can be no greater blessing than to be able to say, at the end of life's long journey, "Father, I knew what your will for my life was, and by your grace I did it!" This is what we need to be teaching to our children. We need to tell them that the most important thing in life is not our will for them, but rather God's will for them. And we need to do all we can to encourage them to find out what that will is and then to pursue it with a passion.

When they are doing God's will, they will discover just how joyful life is. Jesus said, "My yoke is pleasant, and my burden is light" (Matthew 11:30). How many people do you know who are constantly complaining about their work? Jesus said that when we are doing the will of God, our work will be a pure delight. You see, you may be doing a good thing, but it may not be the right thing. When you are doing the right thing, there is a strength, a joy, a passion, an enthusiasm that is indescribable.

Let us, then, do all in our power to help our children discover what the right thing is for them—the will of God that is "pleasant, perfect, and pleasing" (Romans 12:2).

"Abba, Dear Father"

We have seen that the mission of the Son was to advance the work of the Father. This is the heart of the "Age Thirty Transition." Doing the will of the Father was the central feature of Jesus' life. "Not what I want, but what you want," was his prayer.

What should be the place of God the Father in the lives of emerging adults? The Father should be central! The Gospel is neither a Christology (Christ-centered) nor a Pneumatology (Spirit-centered). It is a Patrology—it is *Father-centered.*

The Gospel did not begin with the cross of Christ, but with the Father who loved the world and gave his only Son for it (John 3:16). And the Gospel achieves its purpose, not when every knee is made to bow to Christ (Philippians 2:10), but when Christ hands the kingdom over to the Father (1 Corinthians 15:24).

God the Father should be the most important Person of the Godhead in the lives of our youth! How do we know this? Notice the two cries of the Holy Spirit in believers: "Jesus is Lord" (1 Corinthians 12:3), and "Abba! Father!" (Galatians 4:6). These cries describe the *essential* activity of the Holy Spirit of God and are as different as night and day.

"Jesus is Lord" is an utterance of faith; it involves proper knowledge; it is addressed to people. "Abba! Father!" is a cry of praise; it involves proper worship; it is addressed to God at the deepest level of our Christianity—*our prayer lives.*

Paul's point in these passages is profoundly simple. He is saying that apart from the Holy Spirit of God we could never confess Jesus as Lord. Paul adds, however, that the Spirit's work is to move us beyond proper theology to adoration, worship, and proper experience! Jesus came to this earth to give us a realized relationship with God as our Father: "Through him, both of us have access to the Father in one Spirit" (Ephesians 2:18).

Let us, then, explore in a little more detail what it means to cry "Abba! Father!"? These words were first uttered in a society whose idea of fatherhood is drastically different from ours. Jesus' story about the Prodigal Son is a case in point (Luke 15:11-32). In Jesus' day the normal relationship of a son to his father was one of life-long dependence. So, in Jesus' story, the elder son stays at home with his father, works the farm under his direction, and remains under his unquestioned obedience as long as the father lives. In Jewish culture, the father was the sovereign protector of his children all of his life. For us, the sign of maturity is the departure of a grown son from under the parental roof!

The father in the Bible is not the indulgent daddy of the twentieth century. He is the one who has authoritative rights to the obedience of his children. Jesus apparently accepted this concept of fatherhood and affirmed it in his teaching.

The uniqueness of the relationship Jesus enjoyed with his heavenly Father is seen in the word he used to describe it. "Abba" is not Hebrew (the language of the temple and the synagogue) but Aramaic (the language of the home and everyday life). Both small children and adults called their father "Abba." The term always bore a sense of reverence. It is not so much "Daddy" (a modern sentimentalism) as "Dear Father"—"Dear" retaining the sense of intimacy, and "Father" the sense of respectful distance.

In short, "Abba" is the intimate word of a family circle in which obedient reverence is at the heart of the relationship. To cry "Abba" implies a willingness to obey the Father's will—at any cost. To cry "Abba" is to follow Jesus into the Garden of Gethsemane, into Pilate's Hall, and up a hill called Calvary. To cry "Abba" means obedience or it means nothing at all!

In the book *Lee: The Last Years*, Charles Flood provides a poignant illustration of a son's obedience to his father. At the Battle of Sharpsburg (Antietam), the bloodiest single day of the Civil War, General Robert E. Lee had a chance encounter with his son Rob, a Confederate artillery man. Rob, covered with sweat and dirt, was not immediately recognized by his father. Lee had been telling Rob's captain to take whatever men he had left back into the desperate fight that was raging a few hundred yards away. Meanwhile, Rob had gone up to speak with his father. When Lee saw who he was, he expressed his relief that his son was unhurt. Rob then asked, "General, are you going to send us in again?" "Yes, my son," Lee replied. "You all must do everything you can to help drive these people back." Rob then returned to the battle.[29]

Jesus' obedience to the Father resulted from a similar sense of respect and loyalty. This kind of obedience stems from a personal relationship to God, not from a code of impersonal regulations. It is not, "Lord, help me to apply these principles to my everyday life." It is not an attempt to conform myself to some abstract ethical platitude. Instead, true obedience is a response to the Father's love. It is *enabled* as well as required. It arises out of an ongoing relationship to God as a loving Father.

---

[29]Charles Flood, *Lee: The Last Years* (Boston: Houghton Mifflin, 1981) p. 48.

Today we need to rediscover the true meaning of "Abba." We need to stop thinking of a Father who says "Come and I will give you whatever you want" and face up to the real Father, who says "Come and I will send you wherever I choose." We need to be ready to become a corn of wheat that falls into the ground and dies in the belief that somehow this is the way to bring forth fruit. We need to re-discover the essence of prayer: *Getting so deeply into God's heart that we pray his will back to him.*

To see the place of the Father in our lives is to free us from our obsession with our own needs to a commitment to do whatever the Father wants. This is exactly how our children need to see God.

How do they do that? By recognizing Jesus as Lord is the first step. Christ is sovereign and supreme in the universe. To accept him as Savior and Lord is to accept his gift of salvation and eternal life.

But it's another matter entirely to accept God as Father. It is to look beyond one's earthly father and to see God. It is to acknowledge that he provides for our needs (Matthew 6:25-34), that he protects us from harm (Psalm 139:5), that he has adopted us and has given us his name (Ephesians 1:5; 1 John 1:5). These are the Father's words to your child: "You are My child, whom I love, and I am very pleased with you!" (Mark 1:11).

Having the approval of one's earthly father is desirable but not always possible. Jesus did not let the sentiments of his family overshadow his call from God. "Whoever does the will of God is my brother and sister and mother," he said. (Mark 3:35)

So let your children know that the Father is still looking for obedient sons and daughters.

Help them to cry out with Philip: "Lord, show us the Father, and that will satisfy us." (John 14:8)

Remind them that the challenge to leave one's family for something greater was issued by One who kissed his own mother goodbye in the doorway.

Favor with People

Jesus was not only rightly related to his heavenly Father; he was properly related to people also. He not only enjoyed the favor of God; he had a winsomeness that made all life seem brighter to those whom he met. He grew up "in favor with... people," says Luke. (Luke 2:52)

Let's take a closer look at this balanced relationship.

Jesus was a *spiritual* person. Essentially, spirituality is a personal response to and growth in God. However, this response to God takes place in the context of corporate prayer, worship, and service to others. In the midst of society, we are called to live out and proclaim the saving power of Christ through meaningful ministry.

While my son Nathan and I were working on our garden the other day, we had the opportunity to witness to a young Mexican day laborer we had hired. This man had been so touched by Nathan's kindness and helpfulness that he was almost moved to tears. As he began to bare his soul to us, we urged him to respond openly and totally to Jesus' call to "come, follow Me." What impressed me most was the way Nathan shared his faith in Christ—genuinely, unconsciously (unaware he was "witnessing"), and with genuine compassion.

We are sometimes tempted to think that Jesus was separated from people generally, that he had a sort of formal piety about him, that he made enemies easily. Of course, this is partly true. In some quarters he encountered the implacable hatred of others, especially that of the Pharisees. But it is equally true that "the common people heard him gladly" (Mark 12:37). Jesus was rarely somber or sad. He was a man of joy who attended weddings and feasts. His friendliness and cheer were known by all, and it was only by exaggerating his zest for life that his enemies could slander him (cf. Matthew 11:19).

Sometimes parents make the mistake of the Pharisees. They suppose that there should exist a vast gulf between religion and the cheerful enjoyment of life. They make Christianity a drab and dreary thing, as if true religion had nothing to do with such everyday matters as establishing and maintaining warn human contacts.

How anti-Christian such thinking is! The Christian faith is not a tedious chore. It is not designed to weigh us down with unnecessary rules and regulations. It is a light yoke that fits well, adapted to our needs. Jesus eagerly gave himself to those he loved, and so should his followers. The early members of the Society of Friends established a rule of life to share themselves an hour daily in relaxed conversation with their household. Such mindfulness to one's relationship with others is true Christianity. W. R. Bowie puts it well:

> It has been rightly said that not much credit can be given to any man's religion whose very dog and cat are not the better for it. How much more, then, ought human beings, and especially all the near and dear circle of a home, to be the better for it?[30]

Notice again: Jesus grew up in favor with *people (including adults)*. Perhaps the most dangerous myth about parenting is that children must be around other youngsters to become "socialized." The truth is that socialization has little or nothing to do with a given age-grade group. What

---

[30]W. R. Bowie, *Interpreter's Bible* (Vol. 8; Nashville: Abingdon, 1952) p. 69.

youngsters need most of all are good models: adults, espe-cially parents, who exemplify the values they should acquire and who are concerned enough to help them develop these qualities. What they do *not* need is the negative socialization so prevalent in today's schools and sports groups—the ridi-cule, the violence, the "me-first" attitude. In short, while young people often concentrate their relational energy on their peers, it is their relationship with their parents and other significant adults that leaves the most permanent mark on the persons they are becoming.[31]

In a warm home environment, true socialization is likely to be a hundred times more effective than in the typical classroom. Young people need significant interaction with supportive adults in order to become secure adults them-selves. An environment with too few adults not only pro-duces children who are more active, but also less coopera-tive, more distracted, more egocentric, and more child-oriented than adult-oriented. If "favor with people" is im-portant to you, keep the home fires lit!

---

[31] A recent study by the Carnegie Corporation confirms the importance of adult supervision of our nation's youth. The report, which focuses on children age 10 to 14, concludes that early adolescence in America is characterized by disease, ignorance, crime, violence, alienation, and hatred. The report's conclusion? "The answer is to provide young people with close relationships with dependable adults." See "Youth Adrift, at Risk in U.S., Study Warns," in *Los Angeles Times*, Thursday, October 12, 1995, A1 and A14.

Chapter 7: CELEBRATING YOUR CHILD'S PASSAGE INTO ADULTHOOD

Developing Your Own Rite of Passage

In Jewish society the proper growth of a child required a community-ordained celebration. This rite of passage was not left to chance but was carefully planned out. Its significance in the life of a Jewish child cannot be over-emphasized.

How is it in American churches that a child is called out into adulthood? Few of our churches have anything that even remotely comes close to a *bar mitzvah* ritual. Most Christian parents have not even considered having a ceremony of this kind. Of course, the ceremony itself is not the important thing. What is important is that there be some point at which young people are recognized as adults and are summoned to live responsibly before God and others. They need to know that they are no longer children but are responsible individuals.

Because our culture has no "adulthood ceremony," some Christian leaders have sought to create rituals based on pagan initiation rites. For example, in his book *Healing the Masculine Soul*, Gordon Dalbey suggests a Christian initiation rite based on a Nigerian ritual.

In Nigerian society, a boy lives with his mother until he reaches the proper age, usually about eleven. Then, one evening the village elders and the boy's father (who lives in his own home) appear outside the mother's hut. They are accompanied by a drummer and a man with a large mask over his head. Their duty is to call the boy out from his mother and usher him to the men. At the sound of a sharp drumbeat, the masked man approaches the mother's door and shouts, "Come out! Come out!" This is repeated several times until the boy, on his own accord, steps from his mother's hut into the outside and is "born again" as it were, this time as the child of his father.

After being led out of the village to a special place in the forest, the boy is circumcised and instructed for two weeks. Manly skills such as construction and hunting are taught, followed by lessons in clan history. Upon returning to the village, the boy is regarded as a young man, proceeding directly to the new house his father has built for him. That evening he receives from his father a gun, a piece of farmland, and a hoe, all of which will help him to establish his manhood.[32]

It is perhaps easy for Westerners to make fun of such rites of passage. Yet these rites are important in giving young people identities. When boys or girls begin these ceremonies, they know they will emerge as men and women, even though they are still in their teens. American culture has nothing like this to offer as validation of one's manhood. As Dalbey writes:

> American society can only offer a "driver's license at sixteen; and freedom at eighteen to join the Army, attend pornographic movies, and to buy cigarettes and beer. The message is clear: becoming a man means operating a powerful machine, killing

---

[32]Gordon Dalbey, *Healing the Masculine Soul* (Dallas: Word, 1988) pp. 50-52.

other men, masturbating, destroying your lungs, and getting drunk."[33].

In many other societies, young men have no question about when they become adults. In American society, they are never quite sure if they have arrived at adulthood or not.

My travels in Asia and Africa have led me to conclude that the struggle for identity is almost unique to Western culture. Possibly the greater freedom of choice Western society grants to individuals causes a greater need to develop a sense of personal identity. Whatever the cause, the struggle over identity is clearly a major problem among Western youth, if not in Western society as a whole.

The result is catastrophic. Mass confusion reigns among our teens. Are they adults when they graduate from high school, when they get a driver's license, when they can vote, when they have to pay adult prices at a restaurant, when they can buy liquor, when they can join the military? Because our society has no rite of adulthood, today's young people often look to other self-defined rites of passage. They are desperate for some way to prove to themselves and others that they are no longer children. Some teens see the use of alcohol, tobacco, or drugs as an introduction into adulthood. Others believe having sexual intercourse or breaking a law makes them adults. Still others turn to peer groups, including gangs, for their identity. Even if the group is "good" (such as a church youth group), when the group breaks up, the teen is again left without an identity.

Dalbey offers an alternative to all of this—a Christian sacrament of male initiation. In this ritual, the father and the male elders of the church meet at the boy's house. A male pastor approaches the door, rings the doorbell, and beckons

---

[33]Ibid., p. 52.

to the mother to allow her son to come out and join the men. Accompanied by the singing of such hymns as "Faith of Our Fathers" and "Rise Up O Men of God," the boy voluntarily gathers himself to the group, then is driven to a church campground for a period of discipline and instruction.[34]

Such a ritual of initiation would go a long way toward affirming the maleness of our sons. Obviously, however, for many people this type of ritual would require an unrealistic level of planning, organization, and commitment on the part of parents and church leaders. Perhaps this type of a ritual can also be criticized for being rooted in African culture and not in the Scriptures.

What, then, can we do to help our children embrace true adulthood? With Jesus' *bar mitzvah* ritual in mind, I offer the following suggestions.

1. *Hold a special worship service at church or in your home just for your child, on or near his or her twelfth birthday.*

Invite as many significant adults as possible to attend (grandparents, aunts and uncles, pastors, youth pastors, "adopted" relatives, etc.). Plan the event just as carefully as you would a Sunday worship service. Make it an unforgettable experience for the young person involved.

2. *Review the child's family history.*

Take some time during the celebration to remember the men and women from whom your children come: stories of their grandparents, as well as stories of their physical and spiritual heritage. Include talks by older, godly adults about what true adulthood is, and what their faith in Christ meant

---

[34]Ibid., pp. 55-58.

to them during their own teen years. When other adults share their faith with your children, the resultant blessing will be more than you could ever imagine.

3. *Have the father (or a "surrogate" or substitute father) say a word of "acceptance" and "expectation."*

Explain that the child is now *accepted* as an emerging adult into his or her family, church, and community, and that the adults present promise always to be there for them, no matter what. Then explain to the child that he or she is *expected* to accept accountability for mature actions and to assume adult responsibilities. This "speech" should be warm and personal—an invitation to the son or daughter to enter adulthood.

4. *Close with an act of worship.*

Call the boy or girl forward, have the adults lay their hands on the child, and then pray for his or her empowerment to serve God mightily as a leader in tomorrow's church. Of course, you would then treat the child as an adult from that time on.

The point of all this celebrating is simply this: Just because our culture hasn't developed a ceremony of adulthood doesn't mean that you are helpless as parents. Develop your own "rite of adulthood." Make it clear to your children what you expect from them. Emphasize that maturity does not necessarily come with age but with the acceptance of responsibility. Let them know that, even if no one else does, you expect them to act like responsible individuals.

This task of "letting go" is absolutely essential, but it will not be an easy one. In the animal world the weaning process is rarely pleasant to observe. To watch a mother lion at the zoo slap her cub and knock him away for trying to nurse when nursing is no longer appropriate is a sad sight. It is a painful process to teach him to act like a mature lion rather than as a dependent cub.

The weaning process in human beings is no less difficult. But if we do not call our children into adulthood, if we fail to prepare them to cope in the world apart from their parents, we will have failed in a major aspect of parenting, that of building personal responsibility into our children. And the price of failure in this area is simply too high.

A Love Letter to a Son

Think of all the benefits of a Christian rite of passage into adulthood! In all their pressures, our teens can turn to the Lord. He is their Comfort, their Guide, their Savior, their Protection. When we celebrate their adulthood, we help them know that our love is real, that our commitment is eternal, that we care, that we can be counted on. It speaks volumes!

Your ceremony might include a "speech" like the one I wrote for my eldest son's twelfth birthday celebration:

My dear son Nathan,
When I came home late the other night, I walked into your room to kiss you goodnight, even though you had been asleep for several hours. At moments like that I look at you and think about the twelve years we've shared together. They have been good years, filled with warmth and happiness. There's a love between us, son, that is built on mutual respect and camaraderie.

However, when I saw you dressed up for Honor Band the other day, it hit me that you are no longer a child. You are a younger version of me—the same middle and last names, the same potential for manhood. And Matthew is right behind you coming into his own manhood. Once in a while I look at the pictures of your birth twelve years ago. I can remember how excitedly I rushed into the waiting room and announced to Uncle Bill and Aunt Ozzie "It's a boy!" And now, with the same pride and joy, I gladly exclaim to all, "It's a man!"

It's been a lot of fun watching you grow up. For a long time now, none of your clothes has seemed to fit. Your pants are either too tight or too short. Now that you are twelve, you will never wear children's clothing again, nor will you be able to order from the children's menu. In a few years you will be fully grown, and you will finally stop outgrowing your clothes.

Has anyone ever told you that you are dangerously smart and good looking? Unless you continue to live for Jesus, you will be in big trouble. So be eager to be all that Jesus intends you to be. And in the years ahead, until you spread your wings and establish your own home, I will be beside you, sharing with you what I know of the pressures and pleasures of manhood.

Nate, I really wish you could feel the pride I have over your many childhood accomplishments. I'm so pleased with your HO model layout, your excellence in piano and trumpet, your interest in Civil War reenacting, your love for your horse and dog. I am particularly proud of the fact that you resonate more with Robert E. Lee and Joshua Chamberlain than with Beavis and Butthead, but I am confident that you will never be squeezed into anyone's mold—including mine. Above all, I want to you to know that your human worth does not depend on any accomplishment. Your place in my heart is secure, being independent of your performance.

You are privileged to have everything you need to make it safely and well into adulthood. Not all boys do. As you know, I never had a dad to be there for me, no father to live in transparent honesty before me. Even before you were born, I promised the Lord that you would have a different kind of father, a different kind of relationship. Now that you are a young adult, I have confidence that you will make good choices about life, and that you will build quality into your manhood. Your mother and I will continue to guide you by providing tips on how to set goals for being a respon-

sible and trustworthy person. But the decisions you make will largely be your own. I am giving you a license to wear that responsibility well, to use the godly mind you are already developing and to go for it!

Remember, son, you have been taught that there are absolutes, things that are fixed for all eternity by the will of God. You have been taught that love, obedience, faith, and honesty are virtues in any age and in any situation. If you believe what you've been taught, and try to live this way, you will be mocked and criticized by the society in which you live. May God give you courage to face it!

Since you live, like I do, in a crazy world, things will not always go right. I trust you to make wise and correct decisions in life, but should you ever make a poor decision, I will stand with you when the going gets rough. I will always belong to you, and you will always be able to find me. Unlike other people, you won't have to travel or pay to hear me talk.

The other day I asked you what you thought life would be like for us five years from now. Will we still walk the dog together and talk about things that we're both interested in? Will we still hold jam sessions in the living room because we both love music so much? Will we still go to places like the train club together and dream about the ideal HO layout? Will we still read the Bible together because we know its truths are timeless? Your response was to throw your arms around me and tell me, "Dad, we'll always be together just as we are now." How deep is your love for me!

Nathan, God must love me very much to have given you to me! When I look at you now, tall and straight in your fledgling manhood, I feel connected to the next millennium—through you and your future children. I hope when you look back on your growing-up years, you will also sense pride and gratitude for me, your earthly father.

So welcome to the world of manhood! All of us here today are eager to help you assume the new responsibilities that come to you as a young man. I expect you to work hard to become the best adult you can be, and as time goes on I will entrust to you more and more responsibility. I give you permission to imagine yourself being the person you most want to become, and to do the things you most desire in an adult male. Go ahead and give yourself freedom to explore the wonderful world of adulthood and to discover your deepest longings and dreams. It looks good on you!

With all my love,
Dad.

If all this sounds familiar to you, it should. "You are my Son, whom I love. I am pleased with you!" said the greatest Father to the greatest Son.

Part Three:

On to Maturity

Chapter 8:   EXPECTING YOUR TEENAGER TO ACT RESPONSIBLY

When I became a man, I gave up my childish ways.
—1 Corinthians 13:11 (ISV)

What Do You Want Your Children to Become?

We have seen that creating a "rite of passage" into adulthood is a powerful means of shaping young lives for God. It is a specific time when parents blend loving words and caring actions into a meaningful ceremony designed to leave a lasting memory. Far from being a trite ritual, a "rite of passage" can provide a stabilizing point for the rest of the child's life. Perhaps most of all, it gives children the tangible knowledge that their parents' blessing, and the Lord's, is with them as they step out to face the future.

In conjunction with our ceremony of initiation, I took my twelve-year-old son on a weekend outing—just the two of us. We spent part of the trip at the Prince of Peace Abbey, a quiet retreat center in Southern California. This was a time of learning the biblical basis of adulthood from Luke 2:41-52. It also afforded me the opportunity to teach him the nature of sexuality and how to relate to women with godly compassion and strength. It was also a time to share frankly with my son about my own needs and struggles, inviting questions and observations from him. (Our trip was lots of fun, too. It included the San Diego Railroad Museum and Nathan's first prime rib dinner.) In all this I gave my son a glimpse of how I look at life and the world.

It's the time you spend and the way you spend it that determines the richness of the heritage. The summer walks may seem a bother, the fishing trip too much, but they set the mood for talking—a habit once set that can never be lost.[35]

Of course, my son is not yet a mature adult. But he does embody modes of thinking and acting that prefigure the mature adult mind. His new outlook on life signifies a *capacity to mature*. During the next several years he will continue to organize the behavioral traits that are symptoms of his emerging maturity. These traits include an increase in conceptual thinking and independence of ideas. This is reinforced by the qualities of enthusiasm and zeal, initiative and intelligence, and self-insight and self-control. It becomes natural for the fledgling adult to behave more maturely. At the same time, he reorients his interpersonal relationships. He now wants to be part of the group and is heavily ruled by the group.[36]

Most importantly, during this period my son will gradually establish a synthesis of past and future. It is this synthesis that is the basic challenge of this phase of his life cycle. It is period of self-standardization in the search for sexual and occupational identity. He is looking for a sense of self and a commitment to specific roles selected from many alternatives. At this stage of life, he wants to be heard and seen as part of his society. He now requires full status alongside is peers. Moreover, the ability to reason furnishes him with a new tool to understand his physical world and his social relationships within it. He forms notions about everything from the past, through the present, and into the future.

During this period of transition from childhood to adulthood, parents will do well to ask, "What do I most

---

[35]M. Kelly and E. Parsons, *The Mother's Almanac* (Garden City: Doubleday, 1975) p. 149.

[36]See A. Gesell, F. L. Ilg, and L. B. Ames, *Youth: The Years from Ten to Sixteen* (New York: Harper & Brothers, 1956) pp. 108-109.

want my child to be as he or she moves into the adult world?" Different parents, no doubt, will have different goals for their children. Most will want them to be active in church and community, avoid crime and drugs, eventually marry a godly person, rear children of their own, and generally get along in the world. Some will want children who become adults with social graces, hosting skills, and aesthetic sensitivities. Most of us will want our children to become adults of sincere Christian faith and moral character.

As I write these lines, I'm thinking about my son Matthew. He's only eleven now, but during the lifetime of this book he will grow into manhood. What do I want him to become? Is it right for me to have expectations about him, or are parental desires to be avoided?

The answer depends on the nature of my desires. Some desires—occupational choice or marriage partner—are wrong for me to maintain. Here I need to be supportive rather than determinative. But there are other things I have a right and duty to desire for Matthew.

- I want him to affirm the claims of Christ on his life.

- I want him to discern the true values of life and to be able to live by them.

- I want him to practice the presence of Christ every day.

- I want him to be able to accept himself as God has created him, and to take joy in it.

- I want him to experience the love of others and to know how to give love to others.

- I want him to be an exemplary role model so that other people will want to know God because of his testimony.

Of course, I will love Matthew no matter what kind of an adult he becomes. But I have the parental responsibility of building into his life such biblical values as honesty, self-control, love, patience, thankfulness, courage, compassion, truthfulness, faithfulness, and helpfulness. When we as parents want our children to grow toward the values to which Christ Himself has called them, our parenting goals are valid.

This is not to say that good parenting is a guarantee that youth will become good adults. All humans have the right to choose evil and refuse life (John 4:10). Children can "go wrong" regardless of a parent's education or intent. We've all seen examples of this in our church or neighborhood: the psychologist whose children have deep emotional problems, or the pastor whose children have rejected his beliefs (and him as well). But we can and must use our influence to encourage our children in the things of God.

God said to Jeremiah, "Before I formed you in the womb, I knew you, and before you were born, I consecrated you and appointed you to be a prophet to the nations" (Jeremiah 1:5). God sees each of us as what we are *becoming*, not simply what we are at some intermediate stage. May I ask you to visualize your children as God sees them? Would you take a moment right now and see your children *as they can be*? Better yet, model these goals for them, so that your children will see you live them out every day. They will want to be like you when you make these goals your own.

My writing was interrupted just now. My oldest son just asked me if he could give several old pairs of shoes to the Russian ministers visiting our church. Christians in Siberia, he said, need such basic items of clothing. Since his shoes were still in fairly good condition, I gave him permission, thanking him for being so concerned about easing the burdens of people in need.

I've come back to writing, thinking about the principle of vision I just mentioned earlier. *What you want your children to become, by God's grace they can become!*

Dear parent, your children need to know that you support them, believe in them, are interested in their interests. It is imperative that you provide this kind of support for your children because it is unlikely that anyone else will. Your children need to learn how to dream big dreams. And they will, if you show them how!

Major Areas of Adult Responsibility

We've been talking about treating your teenagers like the adults they are. Now it's time for the rubber to meet the road (or, as they say in Southern California, for the chili to meet the cheese). "A journey of a thousand miles," says an old Chinese proverb, "begins with just one step." Here are some suggestions to get you started in giving your teenagers wings:[37]

1. *Teach them how to maintain a home and yard.*

Teens should have jobs to do, chores for which they are responsible—not necessarily for money, but as their share in the smooth operation of the household. Before adolescence was invented, teenagers were expected to work as a part of the family. Rather than being boarders or guests, they were participating members of the family group. It may sound old-fashioned to use words like *chores*, but young people

---

[37]See also Robert Kotesky *Understanding Adolescence* (Wheaton: Victor, 1987).

need to know that life is not going to be presented to them on a silver platter.

A few generations ago this meant knowing how to split wood and hitch up a plow. Today it means knowing how to operate a lawn mower, use a paint brush, and change light bulbs. It's knowing the basics of cooking and cleaning, and how to sort clothes and program the microwave. Teens can make their own beds, set and clear the table, carry out the trash, help with yard work, wash windows, clean sinks, and a host of other regular household chores. Show them how to do the job you are asking them to do, then insist that they do it properly (Ecclesiastes 9:10) and cheerfully (Colossians 3:23).

Part of learning how to manage a home is knowing how to maintain your transportation. Teens need to know how to wash a car, check the oil, and operate the self-service pump. As they begin to drive, they should assume more and more responsibility in these areas.

Of course, this list will be different for every family, depending on where you live. Our sons know how to care for a horse and goat, but they have never seen a subway ticket or a bus transfer. They know about tending a vegetable garden but not about shoveling snow. But nearly everything you do can help your children learn, and there will always be things they will learn best from you.

Make a list of what jobs need doing and, as far as possible, let teens decide what jobs they will do. One person might elect to vacuum the carpets, and another might decide to wash the windows. Tedious chores that nobody wants to do can be divided up evenly between family members. In addition to deciding *what* each person will do, you will also need to consider *how* and *when* the various jobs are to be done. Letting our teens have a say in what to do and how and when to do it will prove helpful.

Incidentally, avoid making a strict delineation between masculine and feminine activities. The more things your teenagers can do, the more self-confidence they will have. Young women should be able to pump gas just as young men should be able to cook meals and wash clothes. The more your teens are allowed to expand in all directions, the better they will be able to assume adult responsibilities.

2. *Teach them the value and discipline of hard work and to be responsible with their finances.*

During the early years of adulthood teenagers can learn to handle increased autonomy in money matters. Although teens cannot work as they did in the past because of child labor laws, they can still earn money and spend it for their needs. For thousands of years children worked and learned a trade from their parents. Today, teens can clean windows, trim trees, mow lawns, and scrub floors for money.

Some teens start their own business, such as growing vegetables or making crafts. For years our sons have been selling the eggs they gather from our hens. (Recently they decided to give all the proceeds to missions.) When our oldest son turned twelve, he began to mow the yard of our rental property and to help in his mother's office (located at home). He is responsible to save the money he earns and to spend it wisely on clothes, toiletries, train club dues, and so forth. He keeps the money in a bank account and earns interest on it. He has learned how to work with a professional financial planner (his mother!) and to invest for the future.

When teens begin to drive, they should help pay the added insurance costs on the family car. Some parents charge their teens ten cents a mile for the use of the car. Others require them to pay for the gas consumed when they drive. Whatever arrangement you make, make sure you treat your teens as adults by expecting some pay for the use of the car.

We need to teach our children about things associated with work as well. God has a great deal to say about this subject.[38] We need to teach our teens to meet deadlines, to do their work gladly, and to make restitution should they do something wrong. Teens are not too young to be giving to church regularly. In 2 Corinthians, Paul explains that Christians should give proportionately (8:10), abundantly (9:6), purposefully (9:7), and cheerfully (9:7). Even if it is only a few dollars a month, teens should pledge to the church and contribute faithfully, since habits they begin now will continue through life.

Parents should also teach their teenagers whatever skills they have. If you know something about house painting or carpet laying, teach it to your teens. If you know how to op-erate a word processor, teach it to them. My computer sits in our family room. Both of our sons are proficient on it simply because it's such a big part of my life. Let your teens see how you manage your budget, save for retirement, take out a loan, and contribute to your church. Since our culture makes it difficult for teens to learn how to manage money, it's up to you, as parents, to teach your own children.

There will be times, of course, when teens will blow their bankroll early and beg for more money before they have earned it. On such occasions we must be as tightfisted as a Depression-era banker. There will be more money—on pay day!

---

[38]See especially Proverbs 6:6-11; 10:4-5; Ephesians 4:28; 1 Thessalonians 4:11-12; 2 Thessalonians 3:10-12; 1 Timothy 5:8.

3. *Let them make adult decisions—not just minor ones, but ones that will really affect their lives.*

Teens should be expected to take responsibility for many activities and decisions in their lives. They should be deciding what and how much they're going to eat. When they leave home, we won't be able to control what they put into their mouths. So as long as they eat nourishing foods, let them choose their own diet. As long as they get enough sleep at night to stay alert in school and not become grumpy during the day, let them decide when to go to bed. Everything from clothing style to cleanliness of their rooms should be up to them, as long as they take it seriously.

Include teens in conversations when you have guests, and respect what they say. Get their input about family vacations, where to eat out, and what movies to rent. Allow older teens to make decisions about what they study. Point out the advantages and disadvantages of different courses in light of what they want to do, then let them decide. If you have a will naming the guardians for your teens, the teens should have a voice in the choice. Invite your teens to be a part of all family activities. At the same time, recognize that they need to be alone and away from you at times and often will not want to join in family activities. Be careful not to make your teens feel guilty about their need for privacy.

Help your teenagers to make moral decisions as well. Be available to nurture within them a renewed mind whereby they evaluate behavior and attitudes in light of God's holiness and grace. For example, most of what is shown on TV nowadays is brainless mush or gratuitous sex and violence whipped up by mindless producers with comic book mentalities. So when your teens turn on the TV, help them to see the implications of their decisions. Encourage them to ask, "What moral values are these programs promoting? Are such values biblical? Are these programs ones that we, as

Christians, can approve?" If not, make a moral decision to turn them off.

Finally, encourage your teens to make moral decisions about the everyday issues of life. The friends they choose and the leisure activities they engage in are moral decisions, and you need to help them see the implications of their decisions. When they get their driver's license, help them to see that how they drive is a moral decision. Safe driving is to be encouraged, but recklessness means loss of the use of the car.

4. Help them develop a positive sexual identity.

Your teens are literally getting a new body, new hair scattered all over in very private places, and an awareness of their sexual ripening. In the coming years, they will discover that their sexual energy is like a "tiger in their tank." As they begin to take control of this domain of their adult life, parents need to share with them all they know about managing it in constructive ways.

Begin by calling the sexual organs by their proper names instead of camouflaging them with euphemisms. Compliment your teens on being "young men" and "young women." Discuss what they watch on TV, especially the false impression of our sexual identities it often portrays. ("Married With Children" is markedly different from "Father Knows Best.") Never make jokes about the opposite sex (mother-in-law jokes included). Encourage your teens to think through their sexuality. Assure them that their sexual desires are perfectly normal. The problem is with their culture, which will not allow them to marry as teens and express those desires in marriage.

Encourage your teens to think sexual issues through, rather than just simply obeying or deciding not to obey. For example, openly discuss with them the subject of sexual fantasies. Warn them that those who use pornography are setting themselves up for a new sexual stimulus every few days, not for a lifetime marriage commitment to one person. Decide with your teens what comes into your home by way of magazines, records, TV shows, videos, and so on. By learning how to control the sources of temptation, they will learn how to control their lives.

Above all, teens need to regard their bodies as temples of the Holy Spirit and nurture an inner desire to keep themselves pure. They need to know that they can talk to their parents about the sexual pressures they face, and that their parents have confidence in their courage and determination to withstand those pressures. Parents who develop a wholesome attitude toward sex and who, by example, demonstrate lives of purity and obedience to God's commands, are parents who will ultimately see their children evidence the same Christian view of sexuality that has been modeled before them.

5. *Allow them to have a real role in the church.*

Remember that at twelve Jesus, like other Jewish men, began participating as an adult in Judaism. As parents we can encourage our teens to be involved on church committees, commissions, boards, and so forth. These groups should have teen-aged members with significant responsibilities and privileges. If your church does not have teenagers in such groups, work to bring about changes in these areas.

Teenagers can and should sing in the adult choir, usher with other adults, and teach with or assist adults in Sunday School. These adults are not substitutes for parents. Rather they are the essential complementary components through whom our teens can learn what it means to be a Christian adult. Other areas of participation include doing house and yard work for shut-ins, stuffing envelopes, making posters, being greeters for a service, visiting nursing homes, setting up tables for banquets, doing phone surveys, straightening hymnal racks, writing notes to absentees, washing communionware, assisting in food preparation and cleanup, and adopting a "grandparent."

An apprenticeship program is another effective way of involving teens in the life of the church. This program will enable young people to have a better understanding of the basic ministries of the church and will cultivate within them an interest in using their talents for God. An apprenticeship program expresses our understanding that the youth of today will have the responsibility for the church of tomorrow. The key here is *involvement*. The youth learn by doing. Instead of merely listening to a talk on serving Communion or planning a worship service or reading Scripture in public, they are instructed on the various ministries and then are given the opportunity to put what they learn into practice.[39]

We should also involve teenagers in the religious life of the home. Give them a major role in family devotions. Each teen should have his or her own Bible and participate fully in Bible study and memorization. Your teens need to see themselves as a significant part of God's family and as making an important contribution to their own church and denomination.

At some time in their growing lives teens will need to yield themselves to God's plan for their vocation. Prayerfully explore with them their areas of interest and ability, then suggest ways to use them vocationally. Assure them that God has a plan for their lives, and that whatever they choose out of the hundreds of jobs open to them, they

---

[39]For more ideas on leadership training of youth, see D. Roadcup (ed.), *Methods for Youth Ministry* (Cincinnati: Standard, 1986) pp. 151-161.

should use their God-given abilities for his glory. While it certainly isn't God's will for every Christian to enter professional Christian service, encourage your teens to consider vocational ministry as a live option. But no matter what vocation they believe God is leading them into, teens should learn how to be ambassadors for Jesus Christ for the rest of their lives.

6. Help them develop the habit of mature, gracious speech.

"Get out of my way!" conveys a childish air and shows disrespect to other people. Introduce your teens to such phrases as "would you please," "may I please," "would it be all right with you," and reaffirm the importance of "thank you" and other polite expressions. Teach them to substitute "Would it be all right with you if I use that ball?" for, "I want that ball!"

If your teens have picked up negative speech habits, at every opportunity discuss with them the difference between:

"Stop it" vs. "Would you mind not doing that?"
"I want" vs. "May I please have...?"
"Get out of my way" vs. "May I please get through?"

Above all else, teach by example: "Dear, this afternoon Mom was really edgy. I'm very sorry. I appreciate your understanding." "Son, I promised you I would do that and I broke my promise. I'm wrong. Please forgive me." "Honey, what I said in front of those people must have embarrassed you. I shouldn't have said it that way." "Thank you very much. I really appreciate that."

Let your love be visible and audible. Let your positive attitude be sustained until it's an ingrained habit. Privately and publicly, let your teens know that you believe in the persons they are now and are becoming.

7. *Hold them accountable.*

Set limits that are consistent with godly values, and then make them stick, because your teenager is going to challenge your limits. Teens need to learn not only to accept limits but also how to adjust their behavior. By so doing, they find out how powerful they are as individuals—that they can in fact exert control over themselves and their world.

Of course, each family has to define its own values and limits. In one family, importance may be attached to sports or hobbies, in another it may be music or the academic excellence. Some values, such as underage teenage drinking and the purchase of alcohol, are defined by society, which means that they have legal overtones and broader implications than family values.

A curfew is an example of a limit that families must agree upon. You need to agree with your teens what the boundary is, and what will happen if the boundary is "tested." Note that the question is not what the "punishment" should be. Teens are too old to be "punished," but they can and should understand the concept of "consequences." When they test certain limits, they run the risk of suffering certain consequences. By setting limits and reacting to those limits when they are violated, you teach your teens that actions have consequences, and that they are responsible for any undesirable consequences they bring upon themselves. By learning this, your teens acquire a valuable lesson about the importance of ordering their own behavior.

In our home we have a rule that work must be done with a positive attitude. Grumbling and complaining is not tolerated because it is, frankly, sinful (see Philippians 2:14).

If one of our sons persists in complaining, he becomes "slave for the day," required to do anything (within reason) that anyone else in the family tells him to do. The slave for the day usually ends up washing all the dishes, making everyone else's beds, and performing chores normally done by other family members. What's more, he is expected to serve willingly and joyfully, or else his term as "slave for the day" is extended into the following day. The "slave for the day" technique usually works without such an extension.

Now, if your teenagers are like most complainers, they won't like it when they are told that the consequence of their behavior is they will have to work like a slave for a whole day. "You're punishing me," will be the response. "No," you'll reply. "You brought this on yourself with your own behavior. We didn't make you slave for the day, you did."

Your words are calm, and your message is clear. You are saying: All behavior has meaning and consequences. Your job is to get your teens to understand that simple fact—and to accept the limits you've agreed to. If you can do that, then your home will become a place where family values are clear, consistent, and concrete, and a place that you and your teens will share and enjoy together.

These specific areas of responsibility are crucial to successful living, and they should be taught in the home. Parents who train their teenagers in these seven areas are laying the groundwork for future happiness. If we want our children to grow into mature, dependable adults, we need to give them personal responsibility. Applying these simple principles should go a long way toward preparing our children to take care of their needs in life.

Remember, however, that God has created all people as creatures of free will and moral choice. He respects our freedom to choose—even if that means choosing to disobey.

God chastens his children for the wrong choices they make, but the freedom to persist in wrong choices is there. Let us therefore beware of compulsive parenting. Teenagers should not be driven to obey. The Bible warns against parents who embitter their children so that they become discouraged (Colossians 3:21). Ultimately, God allows all people to choose, and so must we. *Young people are free to develop slowly or more quickly, depending on their daily choices about walking close to God, being fed on his Word, and being filled with his Spirit.*

Chapter 9:   TEACHING YOUR TEEN ABOUT SEX AND COURTSHIP

Helping Your Teenager Make a Commitment to Purity

Nothing is more important in a person's life than his or her home or family. Yet many who marry and begin to raise a family are ignorant of what it takes to have a successful marriage. The typical teenage boy knows more about internal combustion than about the mechanics of successful personal relationships.

How old is a person when he or she is old enough to get married? We have argued in this book that there are no age limits. I have known eighteen-year-olds who were ready for marriage, but I also know thirty-eight-year-olds who are not. As we have seen, the key is a person's willingness to assume personal responsibility in life.

Like you, I believe that sex is reserved for married partners, and everything in this chapter will be presented from that perspective. It is also my conviction that it is our responsibility as parents to teach our children about sex and courtship, even if these are difficult subjects for most of us to discuss. Many parents would prefer to let the issue alone. But ignoring this subject could ruin your child's life.

Of course, teenagers themselves are very much aware of sex and courtship issues. In our culture, young people are more permissive than at any other time in American history. Sexual permissiveness is not only acceptable but is actually taught as healthy and normal. On television every year, teenagers are regularly portrayed as losing their virginity—without, of course, getting pregnant or getting AIDS or a sexually transmitted disease. Little wonder that so many of our nation's teens are devoid of moral values!

In helping our teenagers to make a commitment to sexual purity, we need to teach them several things. To begin with, we must teach that premarital sex has many dangers, and, on the other hand, that keeping oneself sexually pure has many rewards. These dangers and rewards are well summarized in Tim and Beverly LaHaye's excellent book, *Against the Tide*:[40]

- Premarital sex destroys their spiritual life. Teens can't maintain a close relationship to God and be sexually active at the same time. Sex is such an intimate act that most sexually active teenagers spend time almost exclusively with their partners rather than with their other Christian friends.

- Premarital sex has an adverse effect on their education. Sexually active teens rarely do well in school. Moreover, the vast majority of teenage girls who get pregnant drop out of high school. Sex has a way of preoccupying the brain at the exclusion of all other subjects.

- Premarital sex can destroy them physically. Promiscuity makes them vulnerable to sexually transmitted diseases (STDs), including AIDS. Some of these diseases, such as gonorrhea, cannot be cured.

- Premarital sex destroys their reputation. Young people, especially boys, talk about their sexual escapades. Teenage girls who surrender their virtue are avoided by the morally upright and receive attention only from boys who want their bodies.

---

[40]Tim and Beverly LaHaye, *Against the Tide* (Sisters, OR: Multnomah Books, 1993) pp. 19-26.

- Premarital sex weakens their character. Saying yes to premarital sex weakens one's resolve, unleashes uncontrollable passions, and destroys self-esteem through guilt. Teens who say no to promiscuity tend to feel good about themselves and are more prone to become people of character.

- Premarital sex circumvents God's perfect will for them. The Christian's body is the temple of the Holy Spirit (1 Corinthians 6:19-20). Therefore, teenagers must be taught to honor and glorify God with their bodies. Nothing prevents a person from experiencing the perfect will of God like sexual sin.

- Virtue, on the other hand, is the will of God for their lives. It provides an AIDS-free and STD-free body to take into marriage and makes the wedding dress a badge of honor, not a hollow mockery. Virtue during their single years will make divorce later on less likely. Virtue will enable them to say to their children that they were virgins when they got married.

Earlier in this book we talked about how to prepare your children for adulthood. The best thing we can do is to love them. Teens who are given large doses of love at home are far less likely to trade their virtue in the hopes of finding love. We should also provide for them loving role models in our own marriages. But we must also talk with our teens about sex. If we don't, someone who probably does not share our values will!

Among other things, we should teach them the Law of Emotional Progression—that spending time alone together with a boy or girl friend tends to move steadily toward greater physical intimacy and ultimately to sexual inter-course.[41] The progression is as follows: being alone together, holding hands, the first kiss, prolonged kissing, "French kissing" (kissing with mouth open), prolonged hugging and kissing, petting (handling each other's intimate parts), and finally sexual intercourse. Once sexual intercourse has been experienced by unmarried couples, it results either in a de-sire for more intimacy (and more and more sex) or a breakup of the relationship. Either way, the results are un-desirable. Moreover, once virtue in this area is lost it can never be fully regained. Your teens need to know that pre-marital intimacy is wrong for many reasons, not the least because is it sin (the Bible calls it fornication) and that it can easily lead to a sinful pattern of life (those who have lost their virginity find it easier to go all the way with other dates).

We also need to warn our teenagers of the dangers of sexually transmitted diseases. "Casual sex" leads to more than three million cases of sexually transmitted diseases each year. Most of these instances occur among persons aged 15-29 years of age, and more than half of these diseases are incurable. The danger of acquiring an STD is one more reason to encourage youth to remain virtuous until mar-riage.

Finally, it is vital that we challenge them to make a con-scious commitment to maintain their virtue until marriage. One of the best ways of doing this is through a formal commitment night, using the gift of a ring as a token of their virtue. This event should be planned for the early teen years, possibly in conjunction with the adult rite of passage described earlier in this book. This is a time for a dad to

---

[41]On the Law of Emotional Progression, see George B. Eager, *Love, Dating, and Sex: What Teens Want to Know* (Valdosta, GA: Mailbox Club Books, 1989) pp. 64-67.

challenge his son and a mother to challenge her daughter to make a formal commitment to God, to them as parents, and to their future spouse that they will be a virgin when they marry. This event should be well planned and carried out with dignity. Since you will be explaining to them the reasons why they should remain virtuous, you will need to be well prepared.

A good setting for this event would be the teenager's favorite restaurant. Begin by telling him how much you love him and are proud of him. Explain how Christians are expected to live according to the standards of God's Word when it comes to sexuality. Talk to him about why God wants him to keep himself sexually pure until marriage by explaining the benefits or avoiding premarital sex. This is a good time to explain to him the Law of Emotional Progression discussed above.

Toward the end of your time together, challenge your teen to resolve in his heart not to become sexually defiled, and encourage him to make such a commitment in prayer. Ask him to take your hand and pray out loud as he makes his commitment, and then you can pray in agreement. After he has formally committed himself to God, you, and his future spouse, you should present to him the virtue ring as a visible symbol of that commitment and encourage him to wear it until his wedding night, when he will give it to his bride as a symbol that he has kept himself pure.

Focus on the Family carried a wonderful account of Dr. Richard Durfield and his father-son night with his son, Jonathan.[42] I would like to reproduce parts of it here. We pick up the story after they were seated in a rather crowded restaurant.

---

[42]See Richard Durfield, "A Promise with a Ring to It," *Focus on the Family Magazine*, April 1990.

"Tonight is your night, Jonathan," I began. "This is a special time for you and dad to talk about any sexual questions that might still be on your mind. Whatever might seem a little awkward at times, well, tonight is the right time to ask. Nothing is off limits tonight.

"If something's been bothering you about marriage or adolescence or whatever, it's okay to talk about it. As we eat through the courses of the evening, I want you to just be thinking about any questions you might have."

Jonathan's all boy. He'd much rather ride his mountain bike in the hills than chase after girls. When we first sat down, he had seemed a little uncomfortable because I saw him looking around. But as we began talking, he relaxed a bit.

My son, who has never been on a date, wanted to know *for sure* what 'the line' was. How far was *too far*? He had a good idea, but he wanted to hear it from me.

"A light kiss is about as far as you can go," I replied. "Sexual emotions are very strong, and if you're not careful, you'll do things you don't want to do. So you need to avoid anything that leads up to that."

For instance, I explained, certain types of kissing are going too far. Kissing a girl on the neck can lead to going much further.

As the main dishes were taken away, I told Jonathan it was time to make a commitment before the Lord. Yes, we lacked privacy, but I felt it added to the significance of what he was about to do.

I wanted Jonathan to pray—right there at the table—but I had to set things up a little bit. "Now this covenant is going to be something between you

116

and God until you are married," I said. "We're going to include whoever your wife will be in this process. We're going to ask God that wherever she is and whoever she is, that He'll be with her also. We'll ask Him to help her to be chaste until the time you're married. I want you to ask God for His grace to keep this covenant pure, because even though you may have right intentions, sometimes things go wrong. I want you to pray and then Dad will pray."

Jonathan turned to me and took my hands. It surprised me that he would be so bold in a public restaurant, but I realized that was exactly what he needed in order to stand alone.

Jonathan bowed his head and prayed fervently. Then it was my turn. Before I prayed, I said "Jonathan, I have something for you." I took a custom-made 14K gold ring and slipped it on his finger. Bowing our heads, I asked the Lord to honor the covenant Jonathan was making and help him resist temptation in the coming years....

My key talk with Jonathan was one of the most memorable and moving experiences I've ever had. It seemed our hearts were bonded together.

As Jonathan and I left El Encanto's that night, a couple sitting at a nearby table stopped us. They couldn't help but notice something special had happened, they said.

Something special *had* happened, and it was between Jonathan, his wife-to-be and the Lord.

Making a formal commitment to virtue is a valuable antidote to the secularists' approach of giving our teenagers condoms. Let's give them a challenge to be chaste and let them know that this is the only way to practice "safe sex."

Guidelines for Courtship

According to the *Webster's Third New International Dictionary*, the words "to court" mean "to engage in social activities leading to engagement and marriage." Hopefully, a proper foundation for courtship will have already been laid in this book. Once again, responsible behavior—according to the guidelines of God's Word—is the essential key to success in this area of life. Yet parents should also set forth courting guidelines for their children. Just as we provide for them food, clothing, health care, and protection, so we need to provide them with the tools they need to maintain their virtue. The following are some practical guidelines for courting:

- A Christian should never court anyone but another Christian. Courting is intended to lead to marriage, and the Scriptures clearly teach that believers should marry believers (2 Corinthians 6:14).

- Young people should choose to court only those who have good reputations. This means they should know something about the person they are courting before they go out with him or her. Just because someone professes to be a Christian does not make him or her eligible for courting!

- Only non-sexual courting is permissible. At no time is petting, making out, or bodily contact allowed. Almost all first-time sexual experiences before marriage occur as a result of heavy petting. Therefore, any activity that leads to sexual arousal must be avoided.

- All courtship partners are to be treated politely and with respect.

- Courting should never interfere with a young person's spiritual life and growth.

As you can see, at this point we have not used the term "dating." This is because my wife Becky and I believe that dating in the usual sense is neither necessary nor advisable. We believe that courtship, rather than dating, is the biblical pattern. Dating may seem beneficial, but it often leads to premature emotional commitment. Moreover, those who date can frequently experience numerous broken relationships that are unhealthy and that make it more difficult to be satisfied with their eventual married partner.

Courtship, on the other hand, enables a young person to focus his or her attention more seriously on the issue of marriage. Thus young people who court rather than date are more likely to be more serious and mature.

Some may object, saying that the dating experience expands the social interaction between young men and women. In our view, however, there is nothing inherently beneficial about such relationships with the opposite sex, especially when dating relationships can so easily lead to promiscuity. Therefore, young people in increasing numbers are deciding not to date during their high school years, preferring instead to court their future spouses when they are financially and emotionally ready for marriage.

One of the most important subjects for young people today is how to remain sexually pure in a mixed-up world. There is no foolproof way for parents to prevent teenage pregnancy, for children exercise their free will, and no one can watch over his or her teen twenty-four hours a day. A parent can do everything right and still be faced with a tragedy in this area. However, the percentage of teenage pregnancies is much lower in families in which the parents have prepared their children for this area of life. Following the guidelines in this chapter will reduce the likelihood of your teens becoming sexually active before marriage.

CONCLUSION

Three Reminders

Clearly, God intends human beings to move from help-less dependency upon their parents into full maturity through the process of stepwise development. Of all the reminders that parents must have about the stages of growth, there are three that are most important.

The first is that the Scriptures themselves are the most reliable source of data about the phases of human development. Christians seem to accept this fact easily when it comes to the study of theology or doctrine. But when it comes to the social sciences—the study of a human being as a person—these same people tend to question the adequacy of the Scriptures. It is popular to draw heavily from the social sciences while practically ignoring what the Bible has to say about human development. What so many fail to realize is that the perspective of secular writers is very limited. Secular psychologists are not treating the matter of human development from a Christian understanding of the Word of God, nor is that their intent. Today there is a need for a candid evaluation by Christian parents and educators about the presuppositions, methods, and goals of developmental psychology. There is also a need for a renewed vitality to search the Scriptures for parallels and possible interrelationships.

The Myth of Adolescence affirms my confidence in the important insights that Christian parents and Christian educators can gain from the Bible as a primary source of wisdom. A major purpose of this book is to help Christians learn what the Scriptures say about child rearing. I have also pointed out some areas where modern developmental psychology and biblical theology do or can meet. My hope is

121

that parents will gain an awareness of the broad scope of human development and how they can arrange their home environment so, as to support the developmental process.

The second very important reminder is that effective parenting is possible regardless of the social status, financial wealth, or educational background of the family. Quality parenting is a matter of commitment to spend one's energy on child rearing rather than on the acquisition of wealth and social privileges. Wise parents take the time to understand their child's behavior and reasoning in terms of the stages of growth, and they anticipate the sometimes turbulent transitions from one to another. They learn how to work *in* the process rather than unintentionally undermining it. It is never too late to begin providing this kind of help and encouragement to our children.

At the same time, all developmental tasks are interrelated and interdependent. All mature aspects of behavior have their beginnings in childhood behavior and evolve through all subsequent patterns of development. This means that the earlier parents uncover the nature and pattern of their child's development, the easier it will be for them to predict that child's mode and range of maturation all along the course of his or her life cycle.

Finally, it needs to be repeated that the pattern of human development presented in this book makes use of developmental phases rather than exact age norms. Children's ages may suffice as general guides, but they should not be used as exacting criteria for judging a child's developmental progress. When development does not proceed as "normally" expected, the fault may lie either with a real developmental problem or with unrealistic expectations of the child's behavior based on what is thought to be "right" for his or her age.

Perhaps the best we can do is to speak of God's *blueprint* for growth and maturation. The problem with this analogy is that it lacks flexibility. If a builder makes a foundational mistake while following the blueprint, the whole building has to be redone. Life cannot operate on that analogy. The blueprint must be versatile enough to build several shapes of life. Parents need to see that there are individual differences and distinct patterns that can be made out of the blueprint to be used in all growth.

Therefore, no guidebook can ever give the right answers to every question parents might have about their own children. I have a wife whom I do not always understand, two sons whom I only occasionally understand, and a horse who is forever beyond my comprehension. I don't always understand myself completely. Our children, like all other human beings, are beyond our full understanding. Each child really needs his or her own book, but so many books would be impossible to write. The more worthwhile goal is to gain an awareness of the larger scope of human development and how parents can work with rather than against the process. The actual rate and degree of completion of each developmental phase varies with each individual. Wise parents understand that their own children must always be taken one at a time, with their own hopes, dreams, struggles, and fears.

In the end, *The Myth of Adolescence* was written to motivate parents to take their task seriously. God has placed our children into our care for but a brief moment. Our job is to mold them into adults who love and obey God at any cost. We do this by committing ourselves to the crucial building blocks of our children's life: roots and wings. Then we will be able to say to our children (Proverbs 4:11-12):

I have taught you the way of wisdom;
    I have led you in the paths of righteousness.
When you walk, your steps will not be hampered;
    and when you run, you will not stumble.

EPILOGUE

Several months ago some city workers planted a tree in my neighborhood. They dug a deep hole, and in it they placed a young birch. Next to the tree they inserted a wooden post. The post stood straight and tall, and the tree was connected to it by two bands of rubber. As long as the tree was attached to the post, it too would grow straight and tall.

Recently the city cut the bands and removed the wooden post. The tree's roots are now deep enough to allow it to stand on its own.

Despite wind and rain, it continues to grow tall and straight, just as the city planners intended. It is a beautiful tree, and all who travel through my city admire that birch. It is a wonderful addition to our neighborhood, and it makes me proud to live here.

A MOTHER'S PERSPECTIVE

by Becky Black

> Unto the woman he said, "I will greatly multiply your sorrow and your conception; in sorrow you will bring forth children; and your desire shall be subject to your husband, and he will rule over you" (Genesis 3:16).

Thus the Scriptures state the legacy of Eve, and for thousands of years women have been trying to cope with that legacy. The first part of God's judgment deals with Eve's relationship to her children; it speaks of multiplied sorrow. Though some claim that this is a reference to the actual pain of labor and delivery, I feel that it goes far beyond these few hours of pain. Just as God's judgment upon Adam and his male seed is a lifelong burden of work, so His judgment upon Eve and her female seed is a lifelong sorrow associated with children.

In most cases, the "sorrow" of pregnancy is relatively mild—some fatigue, nausea, backaches. The "sorrow" of labor and delivery is short-lived; its pain is quickly forgotten as we cuddle the new life. The "sorrow" of raising children, however, is a daily burden that takes many shapes. Children bring financial challenges, physical draining, emotional turmoil, intellectual stretching, and significant social changes. All of these can threaten our personal comfort and remind us of Eve's legacy. However, the greatest source of sorrow in child-rearing flows not so much from external, societal issues as from the internal separation of identity with our children. Our children are never so close to us as when they are in the womb. The moment of birth results in separation of bodies, but it takes many years for separation of identity to occur. This tearing apart is a long, painful process. It is a regular reminder that relationships in the world today are not as the Creator had originally designed.

Coping with this separation and dealing with the pain it causes is a very personal matter, even if it is a universal problem. The Scriptures state that Mary "continued to treasure all these things in her heart" (Luke 2:51), and women before and since have pondered the mystery of the mother-child relationship. When it comes to dealing with the separation issue, in my observation we women tend toward one extreme or the other. Either we are anxious to be rid of the burden of our children, wanting to hurry up the process and get it over with, or else we are anxious to hold our children to us forever, wanting to delay the process and avoid the pain.

On the one hand, we want independence and freedom to accomplish our own agenda; we're tired of the burden of responsibility toward our children, and our method of coping with our children is to deny or minimize the bond between us and them. On the other hand, we want our children to constantly cling to us, reassuring us that we are needed; we want to emphasize this bond to the exclusion of other things in life. (These extremes remind me of how some people want to remove a bandage slowly, fearful of pain, while others rip off the bandage quickly, preferring to deal with the pain in one massive swoop.)

All of us experience times on both ends of the spectrum, but I think our basic personalities cause us to lean to one extreme or the other. Coping with our own personal imbalance in this regard is a lifelong struggle and sorrow, for it reminds us in a subtle way that we mothers are tainted with sin and are capable of doing harm to our children. If we push for separation too quickly, it injures our children by withdrawing nurture and protection from them too early. If we cling to our children too long, it suffocates them and stunts their growth. "Therefore, just as one offense resulted in condemnation for everyone, so one act of righteousness results in justification and life for everyone. For just as through one man's disobedience many people were made sinners, so through one man's obedience many people will be made righteous" (Romans 5:18-19).

Thankfully, God didn't leave the scene after he spoke words of judgment to Eve. In fulfillment of his promise in the Garden, generations later he sent a person, his own son, who would empower us women to deal with Eve's legacy. Through the Lord Jesus, he corrected the sin problem, and we women are now able to see things from God's perspective and respond to life with God's strength. We are no longer victims of Eve's wrong-doing.

The empowerment given us by the Lord Jesus starts with being able to understand and accept truth. A truth with regard to our motherhood is that life belongs to God and God alone. Our children are not ours; they are not even, as many say, on loan to us. (The idea of "loan" is temporary ownership; our children never have been and never will be ours by ownership.) Our children are not meant for our pleasure; they are not our servants. Their purpose for being is not to serve our needs (emotional, financial, societal, or otherwise). Understanding and accepting this truth goes a long way in helping the clinging mother.

A parallel truth with regard to motherhood is that although we do not have ownership, we do have responsibility. Our children are our stewardship charge. One day the owner of our children will call us to give an account of our time with his children. Understanding and accepting this truth goes a long way in helping the fleeing mother.

Thousands of years ago, Hannah struggled with these truths. As one of two wives, Hannah was always in a mode of contrast. The other wife had several children, and she bragged on her ability to produce children. Then, as now, children were seen as possessions. Hannah's own identity as a woman, like many of us women today, was in jeopardy; she had no children to prove her worth as a woman. For years Hannah suffered emotional turmoil, struggling under the burden of an untruth. When she reached the end of her rope, she cried out to God and agreed to surrender any child he blessed her with; she finally acknowledged that God alone owns life. Samuel was born soon afterward, and Hannah kept her promise, bringing him to live and serve in the temple.

Separating herself from her son was easier in light of the truth of her non-ownership. Hannah had more children after Samuel; I suspect that she acknowledged God's ownership of them also. And in that acknowledgment came a maternal freedom and joy that can only be described as supernatural. So what does all of this have to do with the myth of adolescence?

As my husband Dave has pointed out in *The Myth of Adolescence*, the biblical Judeo-Christian view of life's stages is three-fold: childhood, young adulthood, and mature adulthood. Childhood (birth to age 12) is characterized by a close connection with parents in obedience, physical care, and identity. Young adulthood (age 12 to the age of 30) is characterized by continued obedience and physical care, but a separation of identity. Finally, mature adulthood (after age 30) is characterized by complete independence.

Upon carefully reviewing the whole issue of youth in light of motherhood, I have been impressed with the graciousness of the Lord in providing for us women who remain under the curse of the Garden's event. To my thinking, this 3-stage development extending from birth to age 30 is a more "humane" treatment of our motherly needs than the harsh growth pattern of society today. Society at large has belittled the role of mothers for decades; the idea of "adolescence" is against the backdrop of a decline in the es-teem of mothers. The familiar "adolescent" pattern today robs mothers of the joy of witnessing their child's blossom-ing identity close-up and personal.

In observing other families with teens, I usually see a policy of "truce and tolerance" between mothers and their children. How often I was "warned" of unavoidable conflict the moment that my sons turned 13! A picture of impending intra-family warfare was painted. The great adolescent trib-ulation was prophesied for our family. And I was accused of "denial" if I chose to think positively about these years. It was only after researching Scripture with my husband that my so-called "positive thinking" became "biblical convic-tion." I saw the wisdom of God in planning life as he did, a wisdom that flowed with mercy in remembrance of his judgment on Eve and her descendents.

Through a biblical understanding of the development of our children, the needs of us as mothers are addressed. God is efficient; rarely does he solve only one issue at a time. In planning Life to meet the needs of children, he also meets the needs of mothers.

My journey from societal dictates to biblical lifestyle has been in many ways a lonely one; it has been like blazing a trail alone. There have been precious few who presented a model and no one that had a clearly defined understanding from Scripture of these developmental years. Though mountains of "how-to" books existed to help me with the teen years, they offered little from Scripture and generally supported the "time out" viewpoint of society in general. I was basically told to "hang on" until reason returned about age 18-20, just in time to send my child off to college. I was about to run a torture gamut that was "normal." I should adjust my expectations and accept chaos; survival should become my goal. (I was having flashbacks to the counsel given me when my sons turned two!)

Being the child of missionary parents, I have often refused to accept what most Americans accept as "normal" or "desirable." And I am blessed to have a husband who is serious about doing things God's way. His research dovetailed well with my "gut feeling." It remained, however, to me to work out the mothering details. The principles of Scripture need to be brought into the minute-by-minute dynamics of home life. And it is normally the mother who is most intimately connected with those dynamics.

Here are some specifics that I've done in order to implement a biblical understanding of my teens in my role as mother. First, I give myself grace. As I've looked at the women in Scripture (particularly Mary, the mother of Jesus), I see that they weren't perfect. However, they were growing, just like me. Mary completely missed the fact of Jesus' new identity at age 12; she was baffled by his statement "Didn't you know that I had to be about my father's house?" (Luke 2:49). And again, at age 30 when Jesus began his ministry, she forgot that as a mature adult he was no longer subject to her authority; the days of obedience were passed. Though she sent word ordering him to "come," he politely reminded her of his passage into mature adulthood by refusing to accommodate her (Matthew 12:46-50). My mothering is improved if I admit that I'm this side of heaven and will make "mistakes." But like Mary, I must be committed to following him to the foot of the cross and receive his comfort and correction.

Second, I must remember that my mothering job is unique. All women of all ages and cultures have the same job description, that of preparing our children for godly adulthood. But we each have a unique set of working conditions and job training courses. God, the Arranger of Life, has made each of us with our own personal set of background data and personality characteristics. No two mothers are exactly alike. Furthermore, he has given to each unique mother one or more unique children. Each set of mother-child partnerships is absolutely unique. As such, we cannot look at another mother-child partnership and expect to do things exactly as they have done. God isn't in the business of mass production, stamping out exact replicas by the thousands; rather, he's in the business of personal art, making one-of-a-kinds by the thousands. Though basic principles of art are applied to all his works, there are no two of us alike. His creativity is endless.

All of this means that I need to cling to him who knows me and my child. I need to actively search his Word and his Face for personal instructions, and I need to take with a grain of salt advice from others that is of a specific nature. Scripture says that "the just will live by faith" (Romans 1:17). Faith is simply acting on the character and word of another.

If God's word says, in essence, "spare the rod, spoil the child" (to use the common dictum), I'm not living by faith if I avoid punishing my child when punishment is appropriate; my own emotional state or rational justifications for non-punishment are no excuse.

If Scripture says "let all bitterness, wrath, anger, quarreling, and slander be put away from you" (Ephesians 4:31), then I need to discipline my spirit and remove anger or resentment toward my children; otherwise, I'm not living in faith. The "whys" and "wherefores" of the anger or resentment are irrelevant. God says "put it away," so I must put it away. It's that simple. If I'm to function as a unique mother with my unique child, I must have the clear directions of the Master Creator, and I must follow those directions.

The third issue is an outgrowth of the first two: I am "in process" as a mother, and I need to be acting on God's instructions for my unique job. The personal growth and the instructions dovetail into the third issue: God's Spirit indwells me. "I no longer live, but Christ lives in me, and the life that I now live in the flesh I live by the faith of the Son of God, who loved me and gave himself for me" (Galatians 2:20). In plain English, this means that God himself is mothering my children through me! My job as a mother is best accomplished when I simply surrender myself to his thoughts, his priorities, his energy, his perspectives, his agenda... and the list goes on.

To many this may sound like self-abnegation, and that's exactly what it is. The wonder of Christianity, however, is that in surrendering ourselves to him, we find ourselves to be complete. Last evening we had guests for dinner. As I set the table, I planned what dishes would be used based on their purpose. I put a fork beside the plate with the full intention that the fork would be used to get the spaghetti from the plate to the mouth. I put a knife beside the plate with the full intention that it would be used to spread butter on the bread.

In much the same way, God has set the table of society and our families; it is only in surrendering our own desires to his plan that we find fulfillment in our roles. It is preposterous to think of the fork and knife exercising their rights; how absurd for the fork to demand to serve as a glass for drinking! Or the knife to demand an acknowledgement of its free-will in choosing to function as a plate!

Of course this illustration is absurd, yet this is what we, as mothers, are continually doing. Subtly we assert our rights to our Creator. We insist on rearranging the table of our life circumstances to meet our own desires. And then we wonder why the table gets so full of messes, some of which will leave a stain for the rest of life!

No, my sisters, if we know him, if we have received his gift of life, then we must surrender ourselves as mothers and focus on simply being channels for him to mother our children. In this surrendering we will find that not only is our mothering effective, but we are also fulfilled as individuals; we experience a deep, deep sense of satisfaction and thrill as we find our work to be perfectly fitted to us.

When we acknowledge the fact that adolescence is an unbiblical myth and accept the childhood/young adulthood/mature adulthood model of growth, then we have taken a first step toward God-directed mothering. This biblical model best suits the needs of our children and best helps us to cope with the legacy of Eve. For it is during the young adulthood stage that we get the privilege of witnessing up close and personal God's "calling out" our children into their adult identities. In essence, our child's accountability moves from us as parent to God as parent. Though we are still closely connected with our children during this time, we are also on the sidelines, and God himself steps into that place of intimacy with our children.

This overt resignation as a mother is shown in practical things. For instance, if my son is hurting emotionally, I can best serve him by taking him to the God of all Comfort. If my son is coping with a decision, I can best serve him by referring him to the God of all Wisdom. If my son is being challenged with meeting his responsibilities, I can best serve him by modeling stewardship. In essence, I "cease" to be a mother; any counsel or comfort I render is as adult to adult, along the lines of counsel and comfort that I would give to my neighbor down the street. I become more of a mentor and friend. My son now finds in God himself everything that he used to find in me as a mother. God impresses him with the "rules" he should follow; God "kisses his boo-boos" and soothes his spirit; and God arranges his social calendar.

Does this mean that I cease to have any meaningful role in his life? No, but it does mean that my role changes dramatically. "Mothering" ceases, but "managing" continues. In past generations, economic systems and society allowed an individual to support themselves materially from about age 12. Today, however, labor laws and child welfare laws require children to remain at home until age 18. Hence, although my mothering ceases, my household management continues. To this end, many of the functions I do continue. I still cook suppers, clean bathrooms, buy groceries, pay utility bills. But I no longer do them as a mother. I now do these things not for purposes of nurture (i.e. mothering) so much as for purposes of household management.

In much the same way, it falls to me to structure home activities, keeping everyone connected in an operative mode. Hence, my "rules" are limited to those that are necessary for schedule coordination. Sometimes we discuss our activities, and we set appropriate time "rules." For example, each person in our family enjoys corporate prayer before bed; common sense dictates that it's easier to pray together at bedtime if we all go to bed more or less at the same time. Therefore, we've set 10:00 as bedtime in our home. However, it's not a matter of "disobedience" if a son stays up later; it's just a matter of inconvenience. Though on many issues we have a mutually-agreed-upon "rule," on other issues I make unilateral announcements. These "rules" are management decisions, not mothering decisions.

Another example is my grocery budget. My stewardship conscience will not allow me to buy an unlimited number of sodas. So I have announced that I will buy one 2-liter per person per week; if they want more, it comes out of their pocket and will be purchased with their time and energy, not mine. If I were still functioning in "mother" mode, I would set this limitation for purposes of providing nutritional discipline. Now I set the rule for purposes of fiscal management.

As I write this, I'm impressed with a parallel: those of us who are Christians do much the same things in life that non-Christians do. We go to work; we eat and sleep; we watch TV or play sports. But as Christians, our motivation is entirely different; we do it "for the glory of God." We have one eye on him while we go about our daily activities. We are seeking to bring him joy, and though our outward actions are similar to non-Christians, our inward attitude and orientation is vastly different.

In much the same way, though my children leave childhood and pass into young adulthood, I may continue to do much the same activities. But my attitude and orientation are now vastly different. The reasons for my actions have changed from nurture (motherhood) to organization (management). Just as a Christian is noted in the workplace because of that intangible difference in attitude, so the mother who has accepted the biblical age-12 passage has an intangible difference. There is a sense of things fitting and working as they should, a sense of being at home with the Creator.

Each of us mothers will work out the specifics of our calling, just as each Christian works out the specifics of their walk with God. But if we are to be partners with the Creator, we must start with embracing his pattern for life and throwing out the myth of adolescence.

FOR FURTHER READING

I have found the following books extremely helpful and readable. I commend them to you.

Aleshire, Daniel O. *Understanding Today's Youth*. Nashville: Convention Press, 1982.

Cuthbertson, Duane. *Raising Your Child, Not Your Voice*. Wheaton: Victor Books, 1986.

Dalbey, Gordon. *Healing the Masculine Soul*. Dallas: Word, 1988.

Dobson, James. *Hide or Seek: How to Build Self-Esteem in Your Child*. Old Tappan, NJ: Revell, 1974.

Highlander, Don H. *Positive Parenting*. Dallas: Word, 1980.

Joy, Donald M. *Sex, Strength and the Secrets of Becoming a Man*. Ventura, CA: Regal, 1990.

Kesler, Jay. *Ten Mistakes Parents Make With Teenagers (And How To Avoid Them)*. Dallas: Word, 1988.

Kett, Joseph F. *Rites of Passage: Adolescence in America, 1790 to the Present*. New York: Basic Books, 1977.

Kotesky, Ronald L. *Understanding Adolescence*. Wheaton: Victor Books, 1987.

LaHaye, Tim and Beverly. *Against the Tide*. Sisters, OR: Multnomah Books, 1993.

Levinson, Daniel J. *The Seasons of a Man's Life*. New York: Ballantine, 1978.

Lockerbie, B. Bruce. *Who Educates Your Child?* Grand Rapids: Zondervan, 1980.

McDowell, Josh and Norm Wakefield. *The Dad Difference.* San Bernardino: Here's Life Publishers, 1989.

Parsons, Richard D. *Adolescence: What's a Parent to Do?* New York: Paulist, 1988.

Phillips, Mike. *Building Respect, Responsibility & Spiritual Values in Your Child.* Minneapolis: Bethany House, 1981.

Purdy, John David. *Dads Are Special, Too.* Wheaton: Tyndale, 1985.

Rand, Ron. *For Fathers Who Aren't in Heaven.* Ventura: Regal, 1986.

Ward, Ted. *Values Begin at Home.* Wheaton: Victor Books, 1989.

Wilson, Marvin R. *Our Father Abraham: Jewish Roots of the Christian Faith.* Grand Rapids: Eerdmans, 1989.

SAMPLE LETTER OF INVITATION TO A COMING OF AGE CEREMONY

October 2, 1996

Dear friend of Matthew Black:

We are looking forward to Matthew's birthday dinner next Monday. Thank you for being our special guest at this celebration! Becky and I believe that such a "rite of passage" into adulthood can be a powerful means of shaping young lives for God. It is a specific time when adults blend loving words and caring actions into a meaningful ceremony designed to leave a lasting memory. Perhaps most of all, it can give children the tangible knowledge that their parents' blessing, and the Lord's, is with them as they step out to face the future.

With Jesus' bar mitzvah ritual in mind, we have invited several adults such as yourself to attend Matthew's dinner. We will be looking at Matthew's family history, remembering the men and women from whom he came. We will also talk about what true manhood is, and what faith in Christ means during one's teen years. In a closing act of worship, we will call Matthew forward, have the men lay their hands on him, and then pray for his empowerment to serve God mightily as a leader in his home, church, and community. Later, I will be taking Matt on a weekend outing—just the two of us. This will be a time of learning the biblical basis of manhood from Luke 2:41-52, 1 Timothy 3, and Titus 1.

Sample Letter of Invitation to a Coming of Age Ceremony

In preparation for Monday's celebration, would you please consider doing two things? First, would you offer a special prayer for Matthew, that he would see and feel and understand all that God wants him to experience that night? And second, would you come prepared to share briefly, from your own experience, what faith in Christ has meant to you? This need not be a well-rehearsed "speech." A simple heart-to-heart testimonial about the challenges of growing up and how the grace of God is sufficient to meet those challenges would be sufficient.

I sincerely thank you for taking precious time out of your day to be a part of this event. We look forward to seeing you on Monday night at 6:00.

Until then, may God bless you and yours.

Dave Black

SAMPLE PROGRAM FOR COMING OF AGE CELEBRATION

October 7, 1996

The Twelfth Birthday Celebration of Matthew David Black

"When he was twelve years old, they went up to the festival."

Welcome
Matthew's Mother

Dinner
Green Salad • Barbecued Beef • Baked Beans
Corn on the Cob • Potato Salad • Coffee & Dessert

Opening of Service
Matthew's Father

Flute Solo
Matthew's Grandmother

A Godly Heritage
Matthew's Grandfather

Open Sharing
All Are Welcome to Speak

Hymn of Adoration to God
"Great Is Thy Faithfulness"

Welcome to Adulthood
Matthew's Father

Laying on of Hands
Matthew and All the Men

Prayers to God
Matthew's Pastors

Closing Hymn of Praise to God

WHAT IS A MAN?

What is a man, Matthew? Is he tough like Clint Eastwood, tender like Jimmy Carter, funny like Bob Sackett, strong-willed like General Patton? Is he action-oriented like Peter, meek like Moses, quiet like John, bold like Paul? What is a real man like?

A real man is, above all, a *godly* man. According to the apostle Paul, a godly man is:

• Without blame and above reproach. No one is able to point a finger at him and say, "You did this or that and didn't make it right."

• He is respectable, possessing dignity and a good reputation.

• He is calm-tempered, patient, peaceable, not quick-tempered or easily angered, but gentle and considerate.

• He is self-controlled, leading an orderly and disciplined life.

• He is wise, sensible, and prudent.

• He is just and fair-minded.

• He is devout, holy, upright, and well-behaved.

• He is not contentious, argumentative, quarrelsome, or combative.

• He is hospitable and friendly to all.

• He is not selfish, self-willed, proud, or arrogant.

• He is not a lover of money or focused on things.

• He is not an abuser of alcohol.

• He is a good manager of his own household.

• He is a faithful husband, wise and careful in his relationships with the opposite sex.

Remember these qualities, Matthew, for they are the qualities that real men seek to develop in their lives. We pledge to model these qualities before you, to show you what real manhood is all about, to pray for you as you begin your own journey into adulthood, and to always be there for you, supporting you, loving you, encouraging you, caring for you, enjoying you, and exhorting you to be all that God wants you to be. To that end we solemnly commit ourselves as your friends and family.

ABOUT THE AUTHOR

Dr. David Alan Black is Professor of New Testament and Greek at Southeastern Baptist Theological Seminary in Wake Forest, North Carolina. He has lectured and preached widely, most recently in Holland, Spain, Korea, and India. He holds the Doctor of Theology degree from the University of Basel in Switzerland and has also studied at Jerusalem University College in Israel. He has written over 100 essays and 12 books, including *Learn to Read New Testament Greek*, *Using New Testament Greek in Ministry*, and *Paul, Apostle of Weakness*. He also serves on the Committee on Translation for the International Standard Version of the Bible with the position of Associate Editor, New Testament. Dr. Black is an avid horseman and student of Civil War history, participating in battle reenactments throughout the country. He and his wife Becky and their sons Nathan and Matthew live on a ranch near Oxford, North Carolina.

ABOUT THE CD-ROM

This book includes a CD-ROM containing a Microsoft PowerPoint™ slide presentation based on the text of *The Myth of Adolescence*. The presentation is divided into nine chapters for instruction over nine weeks as an adult Sunday School course or as a course for week-night Bible studies. Permission to reproduce the speaker's notes included in the presentation is granted to the purchaser of this book. The purchaser is also granted a license by the publisher to reproduce and distribute the presentation handouts provided that the handouts are distributed at no charge to attendees of any study based on *The Myth of Adolescence*. If a charge is made for attendance at a study based on *The Myth of Adolescence*, the charge may not exceed the list price of the book.

The disk also contains software with dozens of study aids, including the entire text of the International Standard Version® New Testament. The ISV® has been called the most readable and accurate English translation of the Bible ever produced.

The disk is designed to run under the Windows 95™ or Windows 98™ operating system only. Technical support for the software is provided by the software publisher. *Please note that Davidson Press does not provide any technical support for the software; please do not contact Davidson Press with questions about installing or using the software.*

And be sure to visit the Davidson Press StudyCenter™ at http://davidsonpress.com, where you can access the complete text of all of the Davidson Press family of books on line, including *The Myth of Adolescence* and the ISV Bible.

INDEX

OTHER DAVIDSON PRESS PUBLICATIONS

Davidson Press publishes an ever-growing family of fine works by some of America's finest Christian scholars and writers. In a day when many other so-called "Christian" publishers are refusing to publish works of substance and depth, Davidson Press is pleased to offer conservative works on topics of vital interest which will stimulate you to further growth in your spiritual life. Here are some examples:

Worldviews at War: The Biblical Worldview and Its Place in Society **by Dr. N. Allan Moseley.**

Dr. N. Allan Moseley looks at the Biblical worldview and how it fits in with all aspects of our life and culture. Some of his topics include Christians, God and Government; Homosexuality and the Christian Worldview; When Jesus Is Not Politically Correct; the Myth of Disposable People; and many others. Dr. Moseley serves as Dean of Students at Southeastern Baptist Theological Seminary in Wake Forest, North Carolina.

Fearing God: The Key to the Treasure House of Heaven **by Dr. Robert A. Morey.**

A number of years ago, *Knowing God* and *Loving God* became best-sellers. Now Dr. Robert Morey completes the "trilogy" with *Fearing God*. In this in-depth volume, Dr. Morey examines the holiness of God and presents us with a message not heard often in today's churches: it is not enough to "know" God or "love" God; God Himself has told His people that we must reverentially fear Him in order to have a complete relationship with Him. Dr. Morey is the Chairman of the California Institute of Apologetics in Anaheim, California.

Christ and the Qur'an: A Guide to Muslim Outreach by Dr. Gleason L. Archer and Dr. Robert A. Morey

Dr. Archer and Dr. Morey have assembled this compact volume which provides Christians with a tool to present Christ to Muslims. *Christ and the Qur'an* first examines the portrait of Christ from the Qur'an and from other Islamic literature. Dr. Archer and Dr. Morey then correct that portrait by presenting the Christ of the Bible. This fine reference work includes complete citations from the Qur'an in English and in Arabic. Dr. Archer served as Professor of Old Testament at Trinity Evangelical Divinity School in Deerfield, Illinois.

A Person of Substance: Word Studies in Christian Character by William P. Welty, M.Div.

Character must be based on Christ and this compact volume looks at over three dozen character clues, all of which are based on key word studies from the Bible. William Welty serves as Director of The Learn Foundation, the non-profit organization which sponsored the translation of the International Standard Version New Testament.

The Answer Book: A Devotional Guide from the International Standard Version New Testament

Looking for answers to problems in your life? Look no further. The publisher of the ISV New Testament has assembled the answers to your life questions through clear and concise quotations from the Bible. You will love this book, and it makes a perfect gift!

ORDER FORM

You can order these fine works from Davidson Press by visiting our website on the Internet at http://davidsonpress.com or by calling the toll-free Davidson Press order line at 1-877-478-WORD (1-877-478-9673). You can also make a copy of **both sides** of the form below, fill it out, and send it in with your payment to the address indicated. Credit card orders can be faxed to 714-692-8874. Shipping, handling, and local taxes where applicable have been included with the price of each work.

Return this form with payment to:
Davidson Press, Inc.
23621 La Palma Avenue, #H460
Yorba Linda, CA 92887-5536

Qty	Item #	Description	$	Price
	1891833111	*International Standard Version New Testament with CD-ROM*	35.00	
	1891833510	*The Myth of Adolescence: Raising Responsible Children in an Irresponsible Society* by Dr. David Alan Black	23.00	
	1891833510T	*The Myth of Adolescence* teacher's package (6 copies)	100.00	
	1891833529	*Fearing God: The Key to the Treasure House of God* by Dr. Robert Morey	25.00	
	1891833529T	*Fearing God* teacher's package (6 copies)	110.00	
	1891833537	*Worldviews at War: The Biblical Worldview and Its Place in Society* by Dr. N. Allan Moseley	25.00	
	1891833537T	*Worldviews at War* teacher's package (includes 6 copies)	110.00	
	1891833545	*Christ and the Qur'an* Dr. Gleason Archer, Dr. Robert Morey, *et. al.*	25.00	
	1891833545T	*Christ and the Qur'an* teacher's package (includes 6 copies)	110.00	

Qty	Item #	Description	Price	Total
		Subtotal from other side:		
	1891833553	*A Person of Substance* by William Welty, M.Div.	25.00	
	1891833553T	*A Person of Substance* teacher's package (includes 6 copies)	110.00	
	1891833316	*The Answer Book: A Devo-tional Guide from the ISV New Testament*	5.00	
			Subtotal:	
1	1891833316	*The Answer Book* (1 copy is free with orders over $30.00)	0.00	0.00
			Total:	

Payment Type

❏ Check Enclosed ❏ Visa ❏ MC ❏ Discover ❏ American Express

Card Number (if applicable) — **Expires**

Name on Card — **Ship to Address No PO Boxes**

Ship to City — **ST** — **ZIP**

Cardholder signature required for credit card sales. — **Date**

X